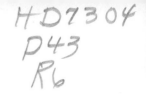

But Not Next Door

by

HARRY M. ROSEN and DAVID H. ROSEN

Foreword by Sen. Jacob K. Javits

Ivan Obolensky, Inc.

New York

To Irma and Frances.
H.M.R.
D.H.R.

ACKNOWLEDGMENTS

To Irwin R. Blacker who said "Do it."

To Marc Siegel and Max Gartenberg who said the right things when the doing got rough.

To Mindy Goldstein who made possible a first draft.

To Joan Irwin who produced a final manuscript with a keen eye and warm understanding.

To Adrien Ringuette, Deerfield resident and partisan, who asked no questions in making available his excellent collection of clippings and documents.

To the people of Deerfield who must remain nameless and who shared with us the expression of their innermost conflict.

To the New York *Times*, the Waukegan *News-Sun* and the Chicago *Daily News* for their kind permission to use the various news articles appearing in the book.

To all these and many others, our gratitude and thanks.

Harry M. Rosen
David H. Rosen

FOREWORD

The barriers of race and creed in housing in the United States are more numerous now than at any time in our history; but at the same time the pressures against a continuance of residential segregation are becoming irresistible. The injustice and immorality of the situation cannot last in a democracy. There is a growing number of Americans—who are Negroes—who will not tolerate being hemmed into slums and being denied an opportunity to obtain desirable housing in the cities and their suburbs. Moreover, our system of free enterprise can no longer sustain the uneconomic aspect of a restricted housing market.

To millions throughout the world, the state of freedom in the United States is judged by the way in which we handle our racial problems. Continuance of segregation and discrimination costs us as much—in those places where it counts—as all the USSR's space satellites and men in orbit combined. To the people of two-thirds of the Free World whose skins are yellow, brown or black, acute racial tensions or violence seriously damage our prestige and raise doubts over our ability to lead effectively the cause of freedom. The embarrassment caused nonwhite diplomats when they are refused the opportunity to rent satisfactory housing in the nation's capital because of the color of their skins or when they are refused service in public restaurants under the Southern "social system" is exploited to the full by Communist propaganda and may well cost us heavily in the confidence and trust of the uncommitted nations of Asia and Africa.

What happened in Deerfield is exceptional only in the sense that it involved a new housing project. A whole sad mythology has developed around the subject of minority occupancy and property values. The uncritical acceptance of the contention that values will depreciate with the entry of a minority into a neighborhood is so widespread and well established that to many it amounts to an article of faith. Yet, there is a wealth of scientific evidence to refute that conclusion.

Investigation has shown that the entry of nonwhites into a neighborhood had either a favorable effect or no effect at all on property values in the majority of cases. If white residents panic and a mass exodus ensues, the expectation of a fall in property values becomes a self-fulfilling prophecy. It is the mass exodus rather than the entry of the minority that gluts the market. The sudden oversupply of houses depresses values. On the other hand, if the white residents do not yield to fear and panic, but behave normally, the existing demand for nonwhite housing may actually cause values to go up. It has been clearly demonstrated that in many integrated neighborhoods where the concern is for good neighbors, regardless of race or creed, values remain stable.

Many of us may not realize that Americans who are Negroes were not always hemmed into rigidly segregated areas—not even in the South. In Northern and Midwestern cities, at the turn of the century, Negroes lived in clusters in racially mixed neighborhoods. In Chicago, Negroes lived in practically every section of the city, and a third of them were living in areas with less than 10 percent Negro residents. In Minneapolis and in Columbus, Negro residents were scattered throughout the city. In New England, integration of the small Negro population was customary in church, school and community activities. During the 1930's in Charleston, South Carolina, the majority of Negroes lived in blocks that ranged from half nonwhite to all nonwhite, but close to 40 percent lived in blocks that were more than half white, and seven percent lived in neighborhoods that were more than 90 percent white.

This is not an untypical pattern in many Southern cities, and even today it is not exceptional in the South to find Negroes living on one side of a street and whites on the other.

During the last decade, many states and cities have provided laws to guarantee the equal right to shelter. More than 49 cities and 17 states have adopted laws or resolutions related to discrimination in housing. The pattern for this nationwide drive was set in New York City in 1957 with the adoption of the Sharkey-Brown-Isaacs Fair Housing Practices Law—the first in the nation barring discrimination in housing. New York State, a leader in anti-discrimination law, is now following suit in private housing. It is worth noting that none of the dire predictions of increased tensions, depreciation in property values or inundation of neighborhoods has come to pass. On the contrary, the evidence shows that slow but steady progress has been made in accomplishing the purposes of the law.

Genuinely interracial developments such as the one proposed at Deerfield are not as rare over the United States as many people seem to believe. About fifty such projects were privately built in the decade following World War II. Madison, Wisconsin; Yellow Springs, Ohio; Minneapolis, Minnesota; Village Creek, Connecticut; Palo Alto, California; and Chicago, Illinois, are among the places where planned, open-occupancy developments have been successfully constructed. In Sunnyhills—a project in

Milpitas, California, with some 1,500 homes sponsored by the United Auto Workers—nonwhite families living throughout the development represent about 10 percent of the residents.

Prairie Shores in Chicago and Morningside Gardens in New York City are among many of the newer developments operated under an open-occupancy policy; others can be found or are under construction in Washington, D.C.; Cleveland, Ohio; St. Louis, Missouri; and Sacramento and San Francisco, California.

A world which is confronted by an aggressive Communism, an awakening and largely neutralist Asia, an emerging Africa and a proud nationalism in Latin America makes the existence of segregation and discrimination in the United States intolerable. We have made tremendous strides in this fight, particularly in the last decade when the need for the sanction of law became widely recognized. But we have a long way still to go, and we have begun to run out of time—hence the importance to our society of Deerfield's welltold history as it appears in this book.

Jacob K. Javits, U.S.S.
Washington, D.C.

AUTHORS' PREFACE

In the last weeks of 1959 the concern of the nation about race relations shifted from schools in Little Rock, Arkansas, to housing in suburban Deerfield, Illinois.

Usually, the racial issue in housing in the North is precipitated when a Negro moves into a previously all-white neighborhood. It didn't happen that way in Deerfield. Not a single Negro bought a home there, no Negro moved in. The tension and drama in Deerfield followed upon the mere announcement of a plan—one that had already been tried elsewhere—a plan to build a small, private development of one-family houses which would be open to limited and controlled Negro occupancy. In the reaction to that announcement, the values of an entire community were put to the test.

The sociologists have ample case material in Deerfield to add new insights to their understanding of community behavior. The courts are already at work deciding whether what happened there is consonant with the law of the land. This book seeks only to tell the story of what happened to the people, to the individuals who make up the community which is Deerfield—how they felt, what they did.

The facts in this book are derived from actual experience and observation, from interviews, newspaper stories, court records, and other sources. The people are real, and the names are their true names—except for three: Danning, Robbins, and Gilbert. They too are real people, real in the sense that they are created out of the feelings and actions of the people of Deerfield, most of whom prefer to remain anonymous. As for Father Parker, Pastor Berggren, John Lemmon, Harold Lewis, the town officials and the many others whose names appear in these pages, they cannot be anonymous any more. Events have already projected them onto the front pages.

THE VILLAGE OF DEERFIELD

You can go to Deerfield from downtown Chicago by any of three railroad lines which connect Chicago with Milwaukee. It takes from forty-five to fifty-two minutes, depending on whether you get an express or a local.

If you are driving, you can get to Deerfield in thirty-five minutes, if the traffic is light. Pick up the newly completed Northwest Expressway which begins downtown not far from the Loop. Turn off at Eden's Highway and continue north past Evanston, home of Northwestern University, and Skokie, "America's fastest growing community," at least until recently. The broad highway ends, and you continue two miles along the old state road to the traffic light at Deerfield Road.

If you should turn right, you would be in Highland Park, a long-established, well-to-do community on the shores of Lake Michigan. But you turn left at the light, west, and cross the parallel and immediately adjacent tracks of the North Shore Line and the Northwestern Railroad. You drive straight ahead a couple of miles through a relatively undeveloped and open section, which changes rapidly to a much more developed residential area. Two or three new church buildings announce the approach of the village proper. Shortly after you cross the village line, you will see on your left a small sign which reads "Briarwood Country Club—For Members Only." In 1958, it was taken over by a group of North Shore residents. Shortly thereafter, the Deerfield Park Board tried to acquire the property and failed when the voters of Deerfield, by a close margin, rejected a $1,700,000 bond issue.

A few moments after you pass the club, you are at the intersection of Deerfield and Waukegan Roads, the business district of the Village of Deerfield, some thirty miles from Chicago's Loop.

Keep driving along Deerfield Road, and a block beyond its intersection with Waukegan Road you are out of the business section, passing under the tracks of the Milwaukee Railroad and entering one of the older residential areas of the village. About a mile further on, after passing a very large and still new-looking development, the Wilmot School and St. Gregory's Episcopal Church, you come to Wilmot Road, Deerfield's western limit. (The Wilmots were among the original settlers of the area and were active in the Underground Railroad in pre-Civil War Days.) Go over the bridge and you can enter the Illinois Tollway, which takes you north to Wisconsin in about an hour, or south in a half-hour to O'Hare Field, Chicago's jet airport. (If you keep going, you will bypass Chicago and arrive 900 miles later at the outskirts of New York City.)

There are some well-known suburbs not far from Deerfield. In addition to Highland Park, which borders Deerfield directly on the east, there is Wilmette, home of the famed Bahai Temple, a few miles to the south on the lake. North of Deerfield is exclusive Lake Forest, home of some of Chicago"s oldest and most distinguished families. To the northwest is Libertyville, a community of farms and small estates, one of which is owned by a former governor of Illinois, Adlai E. Stevenson.

The first settler came to the Deerfield area in 1818. His name was John Kinzie Clark, but he was better known

as "Indian Clark," presumably because of his mixed
ancestry. He settled just south of Deerfield and later moved
to a log cabin on Waukegan Road, just north of the site
of the present Village Hall. The first white settlers came
to the Deerfield area in 1835 at the close of the Blackhawk
War. The right to settle there was a result of a treaty
with the Pottawattomie Indians, and the population at
the end of that first year was fifteen. When the Village
of Deerfield was incorporated in 1903, its population had
grown to 400. By 1950 it was 3,288.

The official village motto is *Aperto vivero voto*—"to
live with will unfettered."

Some of the Deerfield residents of a decade ago com-
muted to Chicago to earn their livelihood. Many worked
right in the village, a major source of employment being
a few large industrial plants. A few stores and businesses
clustered about Deerfield and Waukegan Roads provided
a living for others. And in 1950 there were still some
farms operating in the area.

By 1959, the population of Deerfield had jumped to
an estimated 10,500. There was no new sizeable industry
in the village to account for this tremendous growth.
Chicago's suburbia had simply pushed further north. Every
morning some 3,000 commuters took trains or drove their
cars out of Deerfield to go to work, mostly in Chicago.
Every evening they came back to the hundreds of new
one-family homes in the several typical suburban developments that had been built in the past ten years.

The main shopping and business area was still the
intersection of Deerfield and Waukegan Roads, but now
there was a large shopping center just a block away. Many
new stores had been opened and some of the old ones
enlarged and modernized.

Deerfield had become a full-fledged residential suburban
community. Located in Lake County, just north of the

Cook County line, it otherwise offered nothing special to bring it to the attention of metropolitan Chicago, let alone the nation. Builders were attracted to Deerfield by the large tracts of available land—flat, without too many trees and, at least at the beginning, reasonably priced. The future villagers were attracted by the houses the developers built— a little larger and with a little more land than they could get for the same money closer to Chicago. And no doubt they were also attracted by the thought of living in the fashionable North Shore area and adjacent to such high-status towns as Highland Park and Lake Forest.

And the people came in increasing numbers—from Chicago and from some of the more crowded suburbs. Then, there were the "transients," the junior executives of large corporations who had been "transferred"—who would live in Deerfield a few years and then move on when they were "transferred" again. And some of the "transients" moved on, not because of "transfer," but because they were on the way up, and Deerfield was only one rung on the ladder.

Deerfield is predominantly Protestant, and all the major denominations are represented by the fourteen or fifteen churches within the village limits. There is one Roman Catholic church which serves approximately one thousand families. As yet there is no synagogue in Deerfield for the 200 to 250 Jewish families, but there is a Reform Congregation which uses the facilities of a public school and a church.

There are no Negroes in Deerfield. Nor is there evidence that there ever were any. Rumor has it that five or six years ago a Negro passing for white bought a home in one of the new developments and suceeded in keeping his race secret until the newspapers reported his involvement with the law in connection with property he owned in Chicago. The man and his family moved out, and the question of his true color is still unresolved. But this was the closest that the people of Deerfield had ever come to having a Negro living in their midst.

There is one local Deerfield newspaper, the *Deerfield Review*, which is published weekly in magazine form. Ads, social events and other local news make up practically the entire paper. It is owned by a syndicate which publishes similar newspapers in many of the surrounding towns. Recently, the *Waukegan News-Sun* came out with a special edition known as the *North Shore Life* which serves Deerfield. Most villagers read one or more of the Chicago dailies—the *Tribune*, the *Daily News*, the *Sun-Times*, or the *American*. Some read the *New York Times* or the *Wall Street Journal* which they pick up on their way to work.

The governing body of Deerfield is the Village Board of Trustees. There is also a village manager. The village is divided into two school districts: No. 109 for the eastern half of the village and No. 110 for the western half. These units have administrative and taxing powers derived from the State of Illinois to operate the elementary schools within their borders. There are two high schools, both part of the Highland Park School District, No. 113. Most Deerfield students now attend the most recently built of these, called Deerfield High School. There is a Park District Board deriving its authority from Lake County. The park district covers an area coinciding roughly with the village itself.

Politics in Deerfield, as in the rest of Lake County, have been dominated by Republicans, with hardly any Democratic opposition. Officially, however, candidates for village offices run on the non partisan caucus slate, with only occasional opposition. In the past few years, the local Democrats have been reinforced by new home-owners from strongly Democratic Chicago, but not to the point where they as yet represent any serious threat to Republican control of the village. In the 1960 national election the villagers gave a substantial majority to Nixon. In 1956 and 1952 they had voted heavily for Eisenhower against their neighbor, Stevenson.

This is Deerfield—a suburban community like hundreds of others that have mushroomed outside our larger cities in the past fifteen years. As in most suburbs, the more recent residents are younger, busier with "activities" and with each other, and further removed both physically and emotionally from the real center of the village. The "old-timers" aren't as busy with PTA and fund drives and endless discussions over the merits of one lawn nutrient as against another, but they manage to control the machinery of village affairs and keep it running with reasonable efficiency.

Some people move out, more move in.

Deerfield is growing.

"We're not bigots. We don't go
around calling people names.
And I don't think we want to
deny Negroes or anybody else
the right to decent homes,
just as good as ours. But
not next door."
— Bob Danning

I

In November of 1959 a sorry joke began to make the rounds in Chicago, particularly in the northern suburbs. It went something like this: What is the definition of a three-time loser? A man who bought an Edsel, put in a crop of cranberries, and purchased a house in Deerfield.

The Dannings had purchased a house in Deerfield.

Bob Danning is 39, a junior executive at the Chicago office of a large national company. He bought his house in the summer of 1957 after his promotion from a small branch office in Michigan to a supervisory desk in the regional headquarters in Chicago. He would have preferred to live closer to his office in the Loop, but commuting wasn't too bad. He could drive his car to the Briargate station which was less than three miles from his house, and the North Shore Line train brought him in some fifty minutes to within five blocks of his office. Besides, the distance worked to his advantage—he could usually get a seat on the train.

Helen Danning, two years younger than her husband, was happy in Deerfield. She had pleasant neighbors, most of them about her own age and with children old and young enough to play and be friends with hers. She was fairly active in the PTA and some of the school committees, and in the nearby St. Gregory Episcopal Church

which the Dannings had joined immediately after they had
settled into their new home.

And Helen Danning loved her house with its big, well-
landscaped plot. Of course, "big" was a relative word—their
last house, where the Dannings had lived for four years,
had had a full acre of ground. But a third of an acre in
Deerfield looked very big compared to the tiny lots in some
of the other suburbs closer to Chicago where she and Bob
had looked when they were house-hunting. And the house
itself—a split-level—had much more room and convenience
than anything they had seen in the same price range elsewhere. For $28,000 they had four bedrooms, a spacious
living room running in an "L" into a good-sized dining
area, a big well-equipped kitchen, and a large recreation
room on ground level which made an excellent spare room.
There was also a roomy basement which Bob had parti-
tioned in almost professional style to create a playroom for
the children and a workroom for himself.

There are three Danning children—Susan, age twelve;
Charles, age nine; and six-year old Jimmy. All three attend
the Wilmot School just five blocks from their home. For
them the move to Deerfield had been a blessing. There
were lots of children their own age, there were many new
activities. With Bob earning more money, the family had
more "things." There was an extra TV set just for themselves; Chuck didn't have to wait for his birthday or Christmas to get the catcher's mitt with which he impressed the
kids on his Little League team; Susan had three party
dresses instead of one.

There was an uneasy feeling occasionally that Deerfield
might be temporary. Every so often Susan would hear the
tail-end of a conversation between Mom and Dad, which
would stop when she entered the room. But she managed
to catch phrases like "New York," "more money." Once
she had heard her mother say, "I hope it comes through,

Bob, and that it's the last move. It would be so nice to know we're staying put." But Susan didn't worry too much about the meaning of all this. Worry was her mother's job. And lately Mother was giving more and more time to that special department.

Bob was just about due for the next promotion. Much as Helen Danning wanted to settle down and put out roots—and Deerfield was certainly as nice a place as any she knew—she accepted the fact that promotion meant moving. And right now they could use the extra money. She was a good manager, but somehow they seemed to be having more difficulty making ends meet on Bob's present $15,000 a year than back in Michigan where his salary had been much less. As a matter of fact, it seemed that the more they earned, the more money worries they had. Life had been so much easier in the first year or two of their marriage when Bob had earned only seventy dollars a week.

Moving meant a new house, probably a bigger and more expensive one. They had lost $500 selling the last one, but then there hadn't been much demand for houses in the Michigan town they had left over two years ago. This time it would be different. There were many families in the same boat as the Dannings—the junior executives working for big companies where getting ahead meant moving, and moving meant buying a house in the suburbs. Deerfield was a nice suburb. With what Bob had put into it, their house should easily bring $29,000, perhaps even $30,000. If and when the big promotion came, they would need every cent of it, and then some, for the next house.

The Dannings heard the news about the Progress Development Corporation and its plans from one of the vestrymen of their church, the very day the vestryman himself heard it from the Reverend Mr. Parker.

Joe Robbins and his wife grew up in Chicago's West

Side, an area which America got to know through Meyer Levin's The Old Bunch.

Joe and Ethel went to John Marshall High School. Upon graduation, Ethel enrolled "downstate" at the University of Illinois, completed one year and decided to leave school to take a secretarial job in the Loop. Joe attended DePaul University and majored in business administration. He managed to complete two years and then left school to work in a haberdashery store on Roosevelt Road, four blocks from the big, shabby-looking apartment house in which he lived.

In 1942 Joe got his call from Uncle Sam. For five months he was stationed not too far from Chicago, and on his last leave before going overseas he and Ethel were married. For three years Ethel Robbins saved money from her salary and banked the checks the government sent her. Joe was demobilized just after V-J Day and returned home to his wife and his old job. He began immediately to look for a business of his own, and he soon found a good buy in a men's clothing store on Chicago's North Side.

There was already a fairly large population of Negroes on the West Side. This didn't bother the Robbins particularly. Their immediate neighborhood was still all white and many friends from their high school days were still there. And they had no children yet.

More and more whites, most of them Jews, were moving out, many to the West Rogers Park area on the North Side. The old neighborhood, it was said, was "deteriorating." And it was. Whether the deterioration had begun after the Negroes started to move in or whether the Negroes moved in after the deterioration began was not a subject of debate among Joe's friends. They wanted to move to a nicer neighborhood, to live with their friends who had moved before them. The young wives were attracted by the new apartment buildings and the two-family houses. The move had begun some years before and now *it swelled. But Joe and Ethel were not yet ready to join it.*

Ethel had ideas of her own about how and where she wanted to live. There was a baby on the way and when he grow up—it did turn out to be a boy—he was going to have a big yard in which to play, a yard with trees and bushes and flowers, and above all—space.

Joe's business prospered and Ethel managed well. In 1955 they were ready to move, to look for a house of their own. Many of their friends had moved to Skokie, just north of Rogers Park, and some had gone still further north to Highland Park. For Joe, Highland Park was too expensive, especially now that there were two children— Marvin and Hilda—and Ethel was carrying the soon-to-be-born Joel. For Ethel, both places were too crowded—they weren't "country" enough.

A house-hunting visit to Highland Park brought them to neighboring Deerfield. It was greener, more open. Ethel was excited, Joe was indulgent (and a little excited, too). The Robbins bought a house in Deerfield.

They were a little worried because there were few Jews in Deerfield. But they didn't doubt that more would move in, and some of their friends from the old neighborhood were already interested. Besides, it was close to Highland Park and Skokie, where there were synagogues and people they had grown up with.

A major activity for Joe and Ethel and other John Marshall High School alumni in the northern suburbs was following the John Marshall basketball team in the newspapers. And in 1959 when John Marshall won the City championship and went on to win the State title, the Robbins went wild. They and their fellow alumni went to the play-offs and cheered from the benches in the stands. The star of the team was a tall Negro. "That's my boy!" they shouted, and they were proud of him, as they were of his teammates, most of them Negroes.

Joe and Ethel weren't particularly interested in Deerfield

7

civic affairs. When the first park referendum came up, they didn't bother to vote. They were vaguely pleased that the referendums were defeated, because they thought taxes were too high anyway. In August, 1959, when another referendum was held, Joe finally went to the school and voted—voted NO.

It was in the Sunday paper of November 15 that Joe learned about the Progress Development Corporation's sales policy for its housing project which was going up less than a half-mile from his home, and soon thereafter came the anouncement of still another park referendum.

The Gilberts, Frank and Paula, weren't born in Deerfield but they've lived there long enough to have earned the status of "old-timers." In their early fifties, they have just celebrated a silver wedding anniversary in their big house in the older part of town. They have lived in that house for some twenty years. Both their children—Jean, age nineteen, and Louise, age fifteen—were raised in it.

Frank Gilbert is an auditor, senior partner in a small firm with offices in downtown Chicago. Because he is a careful man, he has done well with the income from his business which never surpassed $15,000 a year. There is no mortgage on the house. Conservative investments in stocks and bonds bring in a supplemental income of some $3,000 a year which pays for Jean's education at an Eastern university and will do the same for Louise who will be ready for college in three more years.

The Gilberts are not particularly involved in the civic or political life of Deerfield. Their social life revolves largely around the Zion Lutheran Church of which they are active members. Both girls were confirmed there, Paula teaches in the Sunday school, and Frank is always serving on one committee or another of the church, usually in some role involving finances. Most of their friends are also members of the church.

8

Except for one brief fling with Roosevelt in 1936, Frank Gilbert has always voted the straight Republican ticket, both in national and local elections. He's not a rabid party man—he just believes that people should be cautious. He reads the small print on contracts and insists that his clients do the same. In a political discussion with friends at his home, he insists on getting out the particular issue of the newspaper or magazine (he saves them) from which he might be quoting. And he believes in looking at both sides of the question—whatever it might be.

Several years ago when a Jewish developer bought a huge tract of land in Deerfield and began to build houses on it, some of Frank Gilbert's neighbors mumbled about Jews coming in and taking over the town. Frank never felt particularly comfortable with Jews—nor with Catholics or Unitarians either, for that matter. But Frank liked to look at all aspects of a question, and "fair is fair." "We don't know that they will move in," he said. "And if they do, they will more than likely keep to themselves. And we can do the same. But we have no right to keep them from living here if they want to."

Paula Gilbert brought the Progress Development news to the attention of her husband. She had heard talk about it while shopping at the supermarket on Saturday, November 14. Quiet, rather reserved, leaning always on the greater wisdom of her husband, it was typical of her that she should tell him the news and then ask: "Frank, there won't be any trouble, will there?"

II

Max Weinrib is the executive vice-president of Progress Development Corporation which was building the houses on Wilmot Road just north of St. Gregory Episcopal Church. He is a fairly young man—44, is married, has two children and lives in Chicago.

Weinrib is a builder. He has been engaged in building construction, mostly residential, since 1947. He estimates the gross dollar volume of the construction for which he has been responsible as in excess of $4,000,000. But prior to the houses on Wilmot Road, he had never built in Deerfield.

The directors and officers associated with Weinrib constitute a rather unusual group for a building firm. They include—among others—an executive of Encyclopedia Britannica Films, an economics professor at the University of Chicago, a free-lance writer, a chemist, a housewife, a preacher.

The chairman of the board of directors, Dr. Arthur G. Falls, is a prominent Chicago surgeon. His purchase of property in suburban Western Springs some six years ago created a local furor when that town's Park Board attempted—unsuccessfully—to have the courts condemn his property for park purposes. Dr. Falls is a Negro.

During the first week of November, 1959, the officers and directors of Progress Development Corporation met at the First Unitarian Church of Evanston. (Not too many days later an infuriated Deerfield resident would shout in a public meeting, "The Unitarians are behind this!") The initial phases of the project were going well. The village officials had approved the plans. In fact, one of the officials knew the architect of the project and had spoken highly of him. Work had already begun on the two model homes. Now the major topic before the board of directors was the question of interpreting its sales policy to the citizens of Deerfield. Max Weinrib had been in touch with Morris Milgram, president of the parent corporation—Modern Community Developers. Milgram had stressed to Weinrib the importance of community education.

The directors agreed that the ministers of Deerfield would be the most effective interpreters. One of the board members, housewife Elinor Smith, a resident of Evanston, undertook to have a sympathetic minister speak with the Reverend Jack D. Parker, rector of St. Gregory Episcopal Church in Deerfield, or to speak with him directly to enlist his aid.

One of the stories that circulated later was that the builders had approached all the ministers in Deerfield and pledged them to secrecy until Christmas week when the plans of Progress Development Corporation would be announced and explained simultaneously by all of them in their Christmas sermons, presumably to have the news break in an atmosphere of peace and brotherly love, and when two beautiful model homes would be ready for public showing and sale. According to the subsequent report, the Reverend Mr. Parker said that Mrs. Smith had asked him to keep the plan secret until a formal announcement was made by the company. In any event, it is a fact that Father Parker informed his vestrymen on November 10 of the plans of Progress Development Corporation:

Of the fifty-one homes Progress intended to build in Deerfield, ten or twelve were to be sold to Negroes.

III

It was a week before everybody in Deerfield knew that Negroes might be moving to their town. Many residents got the news for the first time in the Sunday editions of the Chicago papers on November 15. But the village officials were among the first to know.

Immediately after the Reverend Mr. Parker broke the news to his vestrymen, in fact, the very same day—Tuesday, November 10—two of them called on Joseph Koss, the acting president of the village.

On the evening of November 11 there was a regular meeting of the village trustees.

On November 12 Building Commissioner Robert E. Bowen met with Village Attorney Byron S. Matthews and was informed that Progress Development Corporation planned to establish an integrated housing project. Commissioner Bowen was to testify some months later that the Village Board of Trustees had instructed him to enforce the village ordinances with Progress Development Corporation as he would with anyone else in the village, regardless of the builder's plans.

On November 13 Building Commissioner Bowen and Building Inspector James R. Kilgore visited the two model houses that were going up at 911 and 921 Wilmot Road and found certain violations of the Deerfield building code. There and then the commissioner issued stop orders which halted the construction.

Construction on the two model homes had begun on September 24. Building Inspectors Chilton and Kilgore had made several visits to the site while construction was going on. On a visit during the first days of November, Kilgore had had to call to the attention of the carpentry foreman some cross-bracing which seemed to be in violation of the Deerfield building code. He explained how the bracing should be put in, told him to purchase a village code book, and walked away. He did not report the alleged violation to Weinrib or anybody else connected with the builders, nor did he bother to inform the building commissioner about it.

This information came out in the federal court trial that was to follow the events in Deerfield. Kilgore was asked specifically during this trial whether it would not be the customary practice to report such violations to the building commissioner. "It would not," replied Kilgore. He was then asked, "If during an inspection of construction in the Village of Deerfield you found a serious violation, would you not report that to the building commissioner . . .

a violation which either created peril to life or property?"

"I don't think so," replied Kilgore, "if it could be rectified immediately."

"Did you ask that this alleged violation be corrected immediately," asked the cross-examining attorney, "when you were at the job site early in November?"

Kilgore was a reasonable man who understood the reasonable exercise of authority. "The gentleman is a builder," he answered. "He knows when an inspector asks for a correction, it should be made."

The carpentry foreman on the job at the two model homes was Harry Leibowitz. He had come to the United States in March, 1949, and had been employed as a carpenter most of the time, and since 1957, as a foreman. Before the war he had attended a trade school, but his studies were interrupted by a long stay in concentration camps. At the same trial where Kilgore testified that it was not his practice to report violations that could be corrected, Leibowitz described the visit of Building Commissioner Bowen and Inspector Kilgore on November 13:

A. Between 10:30 and 11:00 they came on the job and they asked me if the bracing . . . if that is the way it is going to be. . . . They just said the bracing is not the way like they want it, you know, and the job stopped, so I asked if we can continue the day, you know, finish the day at 921 Wilmot. So Mr. Bowen said to the other inspector, "Let's go there, maybe we will find something wrong there," and they went there and they ask me about the joints on the garage. . . .

So in the meantime he asked me for the blueprint, so I handed him the blueprint. He saw that the blueprint is not improved, so he said the job is stopped, we can't work no more. . . .

Q. It was not the approved—

A. Not the approved set of blueprints, you know.

Q. Was it a true copy of the—

A. Yes, it was a true copy.

Q. What did he say then?

A. He said that the job is stopped, we can't work no more.

Q. What happened next?

A. Next I left the job.

Q. Did the other men leave the job also?

A. Yes, everybody left the job, even the plumbers left the job.

Q. What time about was it?

A. Well, it was . . . I mean I went to the city to call up Mr. Weinrib and I didn't catch nobody home, and we pulled out from the job.

Q. Mr. Leibowitz, on Friday, November 13, was the framing in place at 911 Wilmot?

A. It was covered, you know, with the sheeting, with everything we just put in—everything; we were working inside on the partitions.

Q. Let me ask you this one question. When the framing in a house is in place and the bracing has been nailed or placed in position, is it difficult or easy to remove that bracing and replace it with new or additional bracing?

A. Of course it was difficult, because all the sheeting was on the walls, you know. We had to chop out all the sheeting and then go in to the two-by-fours to the thing where the bracing is supposed to be, the way like they wanted the bracing to be done.

Q. Since Friday, November 13, have you been working at the job site?

A. I was working two more days.

Q. Two more days?

A. It was an offset for the days when they sent me out to correct the braces, and then Mr. Weinrib told me that he has got to wait until the work is approved, OK'd by Mr. Bowen, and then I went out for another day, and that's all, that's it, I was never there no more.

Q. During those days since November 13 when you were on the job, did anything unusual happen?

A. Especially on the two days, yes, many people come too, you know, everybody has got to say something.

Q. Did you receive any threats?

A. No, I didn't receive any but just two guys came in and asked me, I was there with another guy, "Are you guys not afraid to work here?"

I said, "Why I supposed to be afraid?"

The one guy told me, he said, "If the building will be blew up, just jump down from the building."

In that same trial, Building Commissioner Bowen corroborated the testimony of Harry Leibowitz about his (Bowen's) statement to the effect "Let's go to the other job, maybe we'll find something wrong there." Then he explained about the posting of the violation notice:

Q. When was the violation notice posted on the job site?

A. I wasn't there when it was posted, but I do know that Kilgore went out some time that afternoon and put it up.

Q. And this violation notice recites a date by which the alleged bracing and nailing violations at 911 Wilmot were to be corrected, is that not true?

A. That is correct.

Q. And that date was November 13, is that correct?

A. Yes.

Q. Mr. Bowen, having ordered the men off this house earlier that same day, will you please tell us how the alleged violations at 911 Wilmot could possibly be corrected before the end of the day?

A. I don't see how they could be.

Q. So that the stop order was impossible to comply with, is that correct?

A. Well, I believe that part of the stop order was that the carpenter foreman was to have Max Weinrib contact the Building Department, and if he had done like other builders in the village do, he could have proceeded almost immediately if he would have come in.

Q. Mr. Bowen, you are familiar with the fact that Mr. Weinrib's office is in the City of Chicago, is that correct?

A. Yes.

Q. And that is some distance from the Village of Deerfield?

A. I don't know where it is—I know it is in Chicago, but how far I don't know.

Q. And did you or a member of your Building Department call Mr. Weinrib on that day, November 13, to inform him of the violation notice?

A. No, because we left—we informed the carpenter foreman to tell him that.

The court apparently was intrigued by what lay behind the summary order to halt construction. Presiding Judge J. Sam Perry asked Inspector Kilgore, "Would you have permitted the men to continue on the job had the foreman told you that they would devote themselves to the correction of the error on that day?" Kilgore's reply was polite but firm. "No, sir," he said. "I wouldn't."

One of the alleged violations described in Commissioner Bowen's testimony was the builder's use of one-by-six bracing, instead of the one-by-four bracing called for by the Deerfield building code. Said Judge Perry: "It is a matter of common knowledge anyhow, and the Court will take judicial notice that a one-by-six bracing is stronger than a one-by-four, of the same material. Go ahead."

Commissioner Bowen went ahead with his testimony, revealing that after finding the one-by-six violation, he had had a subsequent change of heart and ruled it adequate—after an additional work stoppage of three days.

But Judge Perry was careful to make clear his views as to what was involved in the incidents of November 13 and those that followed on the building site. In his summary, commenting on the testimony of Building Inspector Kilgore, he said:

> Building Inspector Kilgore testified that he was biased against Negroes and did not want any in Deerfield. He stated that he had moved to Deerfield to get away from Negroes who had moved into the community where he had previously resided. He was the inspector who posted the stop orders and had the conversation with the agents and employees of Progress. The court has no doubt that under the circumstances Building Inspector Kilgore displayed ill temper, was arbitrary in manner and exceeded his authority in his conversations with the agents and employees on the job locations where he posted the stop orders and at other times. In his dealing with building code violators, a building inspector, of course, is not likely at best to be ceremonious in his approach, and his manners and speech are more apt to be blunt than Chesterfieldian. Where discourteous conduct, such as is attributed to Inspector Kilgore, is connected with the performance of official duties, it is no violation of civil rights. . . .

IV

It was Tuesday evening, November 10, when Bob Danning heard the news about Progressive Development. He was just getting into his car to drive to the drugstore for cigarettes when he was hailed by one of his neighbors, a

vestryman of St. Gregory Episcopal Church. Bob waited
for him to approach the car and then listened in stunned
silence as his neighbor told him that Negroes would be
moving into Deerfield, moving right next to the church,
just a few blocks from their home.

After giving Bob the news, the vestryman didn't stop to
discuss the matter further, but hurried on home. Bob got
into his car and drove slowly to the village. At the drugstore he saw a few people whom he knew casually, and he
wondered if they too had heard the news. But he didn't
wait to find out. He responded perfunctorily to a few hellos,
purchased his cigarettes, and returned to his home, con-
scious of being shocked at the news but not knowing why.

Helen Danning was shocked, too, when Bob told her
about his talk with the vestryman. "Good Heavens, Bob,"
she cried, "the whole place will go black!"

"Not the way I hear it," replied Bob. "The builders have
some kind of controlled occupancy system so that they can
keep the ratio between black and write fairly constant,
about ten or twelve black families to about forty white
families. It seems they've been doing the same sort of thing
out East."

Helen didn't understand this too well and didn't really
care. Negroes were moving into Deerfield—that was the
important and fearful fact. She wanted to call her neighbor
and friend, Betty, but Bob stopped her. "There's no point
in spreading the news all over town and starting a panic,"
he said. "It may not happen. Besides there's no need for us
to get excited—we'll be moving out of here one of these
days, maybe even before the project is finished."

Helen asked about Father Parker's reaction. Bob didn't
know. "What can he say, anyway? He's a minister. His
job is to preach brotherly love. But I bet he isn't happy
about having the problem dumped right on his doorstep!"

"What do you mean by 'on his doorstep'?" Helen asked.

"I mean just that—on his doorstep," replied Bob. "The subdivisions are on two sides of the church property."

"You mean where they're building those two houses on Wilmot?"

"That's right. And there will be more going up north of there on the other side of the church."

"But those houses on Wilmot look enormous—they must cost a fortune!"

"From what I understand they will sell for $30,000 and up. But what difference does that make?"

Helen seemed relieved, and yet surprised. "There can't be many colored people who can afford to pay that kind of money for a house."

"You'd be surprised," countered Bob. "There are many Negro doctors and lawyers and businessmen who can pay $30,000 and more. And they only need ten or so for this development."

"Can the builder really do that?" asked Helen. "After all, isn't that a kind of discrimination?"

By this time, Bob's shock had changed to frustrated anger. "Who cares whether it's discrimination or not?" he cried. "All I know is that there's going to be a big mess in this town, and God knows how long it will last and how it will affect property values! It's less than three blocks away! Can you imagine trying to sell our house for a decent price and explaining to buyers that they have black neighbors only three blocks away?"

Now Helen experienced a different kind of shock. "I don't understand you, Bob. I didn't know you had such strong feelings about colored people. Why, just now you sounded like somebody from Little Rock!"

"It has nothing to do with the way I feel about colored people," answered Bob, and his voice was heavy with despair. "We are going to have to sell this house soon, maybe in just a few months, and we simply can't afford to take a big loss. We can't afford to take any loss. What if we can't sell it at all?"

"Well, who's panicking now?" Helen was trying to be reassuring, as much for herself as for her husband. "Of course, we'll sell it, and why should we have to take a loss? I can't imagine $30,000 homes pulling down values in the neighborhood, regardless of who lives in them!"

"Maybe you're right," said Bob. "Maybe I'm getting excited about nothing." But he didn't sound very convinced.

The Dannings spent a restless night. And when Bob met his usual companions on the train the next morning, he said nothing about Floral Park. Nor did any of his fellow commuters. The word had not yet gotten around.

Joe Robbins jumped out of his chair when his eyes fell upon a headline in the Chicago Sun-Times of Sunday, November 15: INTERRACIAL SUBDIVISION PLANNED INSIDE DEERFIELD LIMITS. He called to his wife and read to her with mounting excitement and concern. "Plans to develop a racially integrated subdivision within the village limits of Deerfield will be disclosed Sunday, it was learned Saturday." The report went on to explain that fifty-one homes would be built in the $30,000 to $35,000 price range by Progressive Development Corporation, Illinois subsidiary of Modern Community Developers which had completed similar integrated projects in the East. Homes would be built in two subdivisions—Floral Park and Pear Tree. The article closed with the news that Robert E. Bowen, Deerfield's building commissioner, had ordered work stopped on the two model homes in Floral Park because of certain violations of the building code. But he denied, said the news story, that the order had anything to do with the interracial aspect of the development.

Ethel Robbins stared at her husband as she listened to him read the story. "But what are we going to do?" she cried out.

"We? We're not going to do anything!" Joe answered. "You don't think the people who run this town will stand for it, do you? They'll figure out something. You see? They have already stopped the work on the model houses. And those other houses will never get off the ground!" His voice was now confident, his manner sure, almost triumphant.

"You don't sound worried," said his wife.

"There's nothing to worry about, that's why! Forget about it!" And he left the house to go for a walk on that cold, dismal Sunday morning. He walked two blocks, to the home of a Jewish neighbor. "Did you see the story in the Sun-Times this morning?" he said as he walked through the door.

When Paula Gilbert returned from shopping on Saturday, November 14, her husband Frank was in his study working on some accounts he had brought home from the office. She didn't break in on him—she never interrupted Frank when he was busy. But when they sat down for lunch, she told him what she had heard at the supermarket: The new houses going up near St. Gregory's would be sold to Negroes, at least some of them.

Frank did not react very strongly. It might be just rumors, he said. As for trouble, no, there wouldn't be any trouble in Deerfield, even if the report was true. Deerfield was a quiet town, the people were sensible.

V

The Reverend Mr. Parker had been the first to break the news, and he was the first to make a public statement about the coming of integration to Deerfield. In his sermon of November 15, he told his parishioners about the plans of Progress Development Corporation to build interracial housing next door to the church. As Christians, he told them, they must approve of integration. But also as a Christian, he added, he could not approve of the methods used by the builder in bringing integration to Deerfield.

Later that day Father Parker made his views more explicit. The occasion was a meeting at the home of Charles Rippey, young Deerfield attorney, who had just been named a director of Progress Development Corporation. Also present were some of the village officials, and officers and directors from Progress Development and its parent corporation, Modern Community Developers. The atmosphere of the meeting was calm, if somewhat cool. Morris Milgram of Philadelphia, president of Modern Community Developers, was the target of most of the questions and comments. The village officials made it clear to him that they were most concerned about the integration aspects of the Floral Park project. Father Parker made it quite clear again that he did not approve of Mr. Milgram's method of bringing about integration in Deerfield.

The next day the minister had another go at Milgram and the builders. This time the occasion was a meeting arranged by the builders at the home of Adrien Ringuette, who was to play a key role in the subsequent organization of Deerfield Citizens for Human Rights. Most of the people from the previous meeting were present, but this time there were more clergymen and many Deerfield residents.

The Reverend Mr. Parker read from a mimeographed statement. He began by quoting from the official report of the worldwide conference of all the bishops of the Episcopal Church, more than 400 in number, held in Lambeth Palace in 1958. The quote was a condemnation by the conference of racial discrimination of any kind, and the affirmation of "its belief in the natural dignity and value of every man, of whatever colour or race, as created in the image of God."

"From Archbishop Joost de Blank of Capetown, South Africa, to Bishop Brown of Little Rock and Bishop Burrill of the Diocese of Chicago," Father Parker read, "the stand and record of the Episcopal Church is clear." Father Parker continued:

> Without in any way compromising that stand, I, in the local situation which is the reason for our gathering here tonight, would like to make the following remarks:
>
> The primary reason for my opposition to the activities of Modern Community Developers in the town of Deerfield is that its activities violate the law of love. One may not morally compel love. One may ask to be loved, one may work toward being loved, one may hope to be loved and so on down a long list of verbs, but the one verb that may never in the Divine order of things be connected with love is the word compel. . . . Love under compulsion is not love in the Divine sphere, nor can it ever be in the human sphere either.
>
> Certainly the history of Christianity, and the history of this country is replete with examples of the mistaken notion that love may be compelled or forced. The results of those mistakes and the continuing cancers they create in men's minds and the body politic may easily be seen all around us. I urge you here tonight to give up compulsion, however legal, and work towards your desirable ends through example and persuasion, uplifted and tempered by love.

Father Parker then went on to propose that the builders create an indemnity fund:

> If your primary objective is benefit of mankind rather than that of profit, then the way to prove this is to share the same economic risk that the people bordering your development are taking. It is not equitable for you to make a profit if your action, good though it may be,

causes them loss. To show your sincerity and true brotherhood, I ask you to put your profits in escrow for five
years hence, to be dispensed to those whose property
suffers economic loss as a result of your activity. . . .
If, as you maintain, no economic loss will occur to those
who are the innocent partners to your plans, then you
will take your profits with you several years hence with
interest, along with the gratitude of Deerfield. . . . I
can say that almost without exception the large number
of worried people who have sought me out in the last
week are concerned primarily with economic loss, not
with depriving the Negro of his just due. This is the
critical issue as I see it, and your sincerity as to benefitting
the Negro may well be measured by this alone.

The minister's statement closed with a reminder that the
builders must be concerned with "all God's children and
not merely minorities," and an implied reproach to the
builders for their "secrecy."

Milgram replied on the basis of Modern Community
Developers' several experiences in the East with similar
integrated projects. Property values, he said, remain constant and rise with the normal market, so long as people
keep their heads, and in MCD's developments, the neighboring residents kept their heads. As for putting money in
escrow, he flatly rejected the idea and said to Father Parker:
"You have aided the cause of panic."

Charles J. Caruso, principal of the Wilmot School, asked
whether schools were already integrated in the communities where MCD had built. "We have never gone into an
all-white school district before," explained Milgram, "but
we have never had any school integration trouble."

As for keeping the project secret, Milgram's reply was
candid, if not politic. "If we had been frank," he said, "it
would have been years and years before we could get a
subdivision ordinance."

Milgram and Weinrib explained how the controlled-occupancy policy worked. The original purchasers signed resale agreements which in essence made Progress Development Corporation the exclusive agent for their houses, thereby enabling the corporation to control the ratio of Negro to white buyers.

There were more explanations and more pleas for acceptance of what Charles Rippey and Progress attorney John Hunt of the law firm of Stevenson, Rifkind, and Wirtz termed "the inevitable." Other ministers were present, and they added their strong urging for the Deerfield officials and residents to accept in good spirit the coming of integration, the coming of the first Negroes to Deerfield.

When the meeting ended late that evening, it did not appear that anybody had convinced anybody else of anything.

VI

There were many more meetings in Deerfield on Monday evening, most of them spontaneous and informal: the gatherings of troubled friends and neighbors. There was as yet no organization on either side of the issue, but there were sides. The telephone calls that had begun that day and continued through the week added an element of panic to what had begun as uneasiness. Realtors, and others representing themselves as such, called local residents and offered to buy their houses for half and even a fourth their value.

The stage was beginning to be set for the public meeting on Wednesday, November 18. This was the regular meeting of the Village Board of Trustees, and no one doubted that it would be very well attended by Deerfield citizens.

But first there was the meeting of the Village Park Board, on Tuesday. In attendance were the president of the Park

Board, James G. Mitchell, and Board members Dudley L.
Dewey, Edward J. Walchli, Donald W. Keller, and Aksel
Petersen. There were several others present, notably Joseph
G. Powell, president of the Deerfield Citizens Committee,
a civic organization founded in 1950 and dedicated to the
"betterment of Deerfield."

The minutes of the Park Board meeting on November
17 do not reveal any special mention of the Floral Park
or Pear Tree subdivisions. According to these minutes,
President Mitchell said that "the Park Board was interested
in a comprehensive plan of land acquisition for the whole
district, and was not willing to run an election to acquire
a single site in one spot or another, but if a proposal for
a comprehensive program was presented, meeting the real
needs of the district, the Board would consider a program
for acquisition of such lands."

According to these same minutes, Mr. Powell "offered
to contact local civic groups and to head a committee of
such representatives, who would make a comprehensive
study of the needs of the entire district, and that in approximately two weeks the study could be completed."

The minutes conclude with this statement: "After further discussion, it was moved by Commissioner Dewey,
and seconded by Commissioner Keller, that the meeting
be adjourned to Monday, December 7, 1959, at 7:00 p.m."

The park commissioners and Powell were among the
defendants in the suit which was brought a few months
later by the builders, and Progress attorney John Hunt
contended that though the "purported" aim of the Citizens
Committee study was to "determine Village sentiment for
and against the lawful activities of Progress and MCD at
Floral Park and Pear Tree," its "true purpose and intent . . .
was to arouse further opposition to said lawful activities."
The adjournment of the Park Board until December 7,
said Hunt, "was to await the outcome of such a poll."

Certainly the presence of Joseph Powell on November 17 might have given natural cause for speculation, since he was not a frequent attender of Park Board meetings. Park Commissioner Dudley L. Dewey had been on the board for four and a half years, and he testified that he had never met Powell until that November 17 meeting.

On the other hand, the discussion of land acquisition for park and school purposes was nothing new for the Park Board. The question had been on its agenda for several years. In fact, the Board had conducted two referendums within the past few months for the purpose of land acquisition, and both had failed. Neither one, incidentally, included either the Floral Park or the Pear Tree development sites.

Whether or not the now controversial subdivisions of Progress Development Corporation were actually discussed at the Park Board meeting on November 17 is not certain. Nor is it certain that the possibility of integrated housing projects was in the minds of those who attended the meeting. But the testimony of the principals in the ensuing trial indicated that they all knew about that possibility, as did other village officials and residents who were not present at the Park Board meeting, but were to become actively involved in the growing storm over the projects.

Park Board President Mitchell first learned on November 14 that some homes in Floral Park would be sold to Negroes. Park Commissioner Keller heard the news on November 14, Walchli on November 12, Dewey on November 12, Petersen on November 14. Herbert H. Garbrecht, a private citizen of Deerfield who was to join the village officials as a defendant in the Progress suit, learned the news on November 13, and immediately called Village Trustee John Aberson on the telephone and asked whether he had heard about the integrated project. Aberson said yes. Garbrecht asked, "Well, what do you think of it?"

To which Aberson replied, "I can't say anything to you, Herb. You know I am an elected official, and you know that's not proper for me to discuss."

Garbrecht was not to be put off. A day or two later he telephoned Powell. "Joe," he asked, "is the Citizens Committee going to take a stand on this program?" Powell replied, "Well, I don't know—we haven't had a meeting." On November 15 Mitchell called his fellow park commissioner, Ed Walchli, and asked if he knew anything about the development that was going on. Walchli told him that the "people coming in town were proposing an integrated community." Walchli was unable to recall later what Mitchell replied, and testified that the rest of the call was "just general park conversation."

VII

Wednesday, November 18, was a busy day for the residents of Deerfield. It began with a story in the *Chicago Daily News* captioned, INTEGRATED HOUSING STIRS DEERFIELD, and a sub-head "Eastern Builder's Plan Stuns Many in All-White Community." The article carried several quotes from statements by Village Manager Norris Stilphen, comments not calculated to calm the troubled spirit of Deerfield.

"People are disturbed . . . we have been receiving many telephone calls."

"It is not something that people are delighted to see. It has opposition."

"We are faced with a substantial threat to property values."

"There have been no disturbances and we won't panic. However, people are already cancelling plans to buy here."

The newspaper reported also on rumors that "efforts would be made to quash the project through rezoning or other legal devices." It also reported that some residents and clergymen welcomed the project "as a test of interracial understanding."

More than 150 people, an overflow audience for Deerfield's Village Hall, attended the open session of the Village Board of Trustees in the evening. The Board had first transacted certain "routine" business, including the election of Joseph W. Koss as acting village president. It was Mr. Koss, therefore, who opened the meeting to the audience, following the official adjournment of the Board proceedings.

First, Village Manager Stilphen read an official statement from the Board of Trustees:

> The Board of Trustees of the Village of Deerfield is making a detailed study of the proposed sale of homes in the Progress Development subdivision on a so-called integrated basis. It is evident from the great number of telephone calls and visits to members of the Board and to the Village Hall that the people of the community are gravely concerned. The people are demanding that action be taken to maintain their property values and the social fabric of the Village. The Board asks and will continue to ask for a calm and considered approach to this problem that it may be resolved in a manner both legal and conducive to the continuance of Deerfield as a fine place in which to live and bring up children.

As far as the rest of the meeting was concerned, the "calm and considered approach" ended with the appeal for it. Many of the people shouted for the village trustees to stop the integration or at least to take a stand against it. But the trustees, led by President Koss, would not be put on the spot. They were ready to listen to any "helpful" suggestions that the citizens might offer. Their role was to "study" the situation.

The Reverend Mr. Paul V. Berggren of Zion Lutheran

Church, one of several clergymen present, warned that Deerfield would become "another Little Rock" unless it faced the prospect of racial integration as "mature, adult people." There was a wave of muttered disapproval and some jeers. "There is nothing we can do . . . there is no violation of the law," continued the pastor. "We are the city which was picked for the project." One resident, who lives on Wilmot Road directly across the street from the development, answered him. "I have been chosen to live across from the model homes. I'm stuck. A good real estate agent won't even talk to me."

The Reverend Mr. Eugene M. Wykle, pastor of the Zionist Bethlehem United Brethren Church, took up the cudgels for a reasonable and accepting attitude towards the Progress Development project. "The builders did not come from the East to pounce on Deerfield. Deerfield was the place that this could happen." Another resident, a naval officer, who also lives on Wilmot Road opposite the development site, shouted back, "We've been outmaneuvered. There's no use calling it anything else. It looks like we are stuck." Someone else yelled, "I think we were euchred into something. There should have been some advance warning."

A woman got up and announced that petitions would be printed. One would ask the Village Board and the Park Board to condemn the two Progress sites for park purposes. The other petition would be directed at the builder. "The president of this organization [Milgram] . . . made a statement saying that if the village really did not want us, and did not welcome us, he would not come. Well," she said, "this will tell them we do not welcome them."

The petitions never materialized, but hope was born in the hearts of most of the people as they left the meeting, hope that the project could be stopped.

For the few residents who had attempted unsuccessfully to get a hearing for the ministers, the possibility of land

condemnation as a means of stopping the integration project made them consider for the first time the need for
organized efforts in behalf of the Floral Park and Pear Tree
developments. They were not sure that the organization
of the opposition had not already begun. Certainly the
meeting they had just left gave ample evidence that an
organized opposition to the developments could count on
enthusiastic support.

VIII

Bob Danning did not attend the meeting at the Village
Hall. He was out of town on company business, and didn't
get home until midnight. But he heard about it on the train
the next morning, and was glad he had decided not to
change his business appointment. His fears about losing
money on his house had become a nagging obsession, and
he was the type that liked to be miserable alone, not in
public.

Joe Robbins didn't go to the meeting because he didn't
want to be involved. It was none of his business, and he
persistently proclaimed the ability of the village officials
and the old-timers to deal with the situation. He got the
story about what had happened at the meeting from the
Chicago Daily News the next day. What he read didn't
make him happy. He had hoped for more positive action
by the village trustees. The idea of citizens' action did not
appeal to him. It might force him to take a stand.

Frank Gilbert didn't attend the meeting because he just
didn't go to public meetings. He had his own ideas about
civic responsibility, and one of them was that citizens
ought to have confidence in their elected officials (although not for the same reasons as Joe Robbins). He was

very surprised, though, to hear that the meeting had had
an angry tone, and shocked at the idea that ministers,
particularly his own pastor, had been received with such
lack of respect. But he was sure the whole story was
exaggerated and dismissed it from his mind. At least he
tried.

IX

Deerfield wasn't front-page news yet in the Chicago
newspapers, but every one of them was beginning to carry
daily items on what might turn out to be the first break-
through of integrated housing in Chicago's northern
suburbs. The papers of Thursday, November 19, carried
the story of the previous night's Village Board meeting in
some detail. An attitude was beginning to emerge, and the
point of view was to become more evident in the next
few days, both in the news columns and the editorial pages.
The dailies were supporting integration in Deerfield.

The same Thursday morning after the Village Board
meeting, the *Deerfield Review* was received by its numerous subscribers. Because it is a weekly, it could not possibly have carried the story of the Wednesday night Board
meeting, but this issue did report the meetings of Sunday
and Monday and the plans of Progress Development
Corporation for Floral Park. The stories were anything but
sympathetic to the builders. They emphasized "grave concern and opposition" by the majority of residents, the
"secrecy" of the builders and the fact that when the integrated aspect of the development did become known, the
news came from sources other than the builders.

One of the *Deerfield Review* stories of November 18
quoted Charles Rippey, a resident, as saying: "I am proud
to be a member of the board of directors of PDC. It
can't be run out of Deerfield. It will not be pushed out by

some lower court. It will be appealed and appealed. It cannot fail. How soon will Deerfield accept it?" The story goes on without a break to say: "Milgram contributed to this train of thought with his statement, 'It is not a question of, Is there going to be an integrated development in Deerfield, there is.' "

Anger and resentment were beginning to build up in Deerfield, but the target of these emotions was, for the moment, somewhat impersonal. Certainly the anger was not directed as yet at anybody in Deerfield. The potential villains were Milgram, Weinrib and Hunt, who were thus far the principal spokesmen for the builders. They were in fact the builders, and they were all outsiders. (For some, Adlai Stevenson was a villain, too, although he could not really be considered an outsider, residing as he did in nearby Libertyville. But he was John Hunt's boss.) Milgram was beginning to emerge as a personality from word-of-mouth reports of his talks at meetings and from newspaper stories about him, including a vignette in the *Daily News* of November 23 captioned "Johnny Appleseed in Deerfield." For the moment, at least, Morris Milgram was a natural villain and an object of resentment: president of the parent corporation of Progress, portrayed in the press—and by himself—as dedicated to establishing integrated housing wherever he could in the United States, an outsider from the East—he was, for many Deerfield residents, the logical person to blame for all the unrest and disturbance and disruption of the calm of this quiet suburb.

In the federal court trial, one of the attorneys for the defense, George B. Christensen, tried hard to establish the centrality of Milgram's role in the woes that had beset the Village of Deerfield and his clients. He said: ". . . this [MCD] is a scheme by which one and one-half million dollars is to be raised to impose racial restrictions upon the occupancy of real estate throughout the country. . . ."

Later in the trial, in cross-examining the Reverend Paul V. Berggren, Christensen asked the pastor: "You knew, of course, that Mr. Milgram was the moving spirit in the entire affair, did you not, after the 16th [of November]?"

"I knew that he was the president, yes, sir," replied Berggren.

Christensen persisted. "You knew that he was—you saw their literature, that he was the mainspring in the whole movement, is that correct?"

"I knew that Mr. Milgram was the president of Modern Community Developers, yes," was Berggren's answer.

A last effort by the defense attorney to drive home the point: "My question was, there are some presidents of corporations who are more active than others—you knew, didn't you, by the time you got through with that session with Mr. Milgram on Monday night, that he was the main-spring, the main source of energy in this entire movement, isn't that right, Reverend Berggren?"

The pastor held firm. "I didn't make that judgment. I made the judgment that he was the president of the organization."

"That is all?"

"That is all."

Yes, it was easy and even comforting for most of the villagers to be angry at Milgram, for it permitted them to be on both sides of the issue at one time—at least for the moment. Nobody had to be against integration as a principle of American life, and, in fact, very few people pronounced themselves as opposed to the idea of selling houses to Negroes. But even those who claimed to be in favor of integrated housing cried: "Why Deerfield? Why not Highland Park? It would be so much easier there. People in Highland Park are more broad-minded, more liberal."

The image of a secretive Milgram trying to sneak integrated housing into their community, the appeal by Father

Parker to Milgram to "give up compulsion" and his criticism of Milgram's "methods," these provided all the rationale that most Deerfield residents needed to oppose the new development without making any moral decisions about equal rights and loving one's neighbor and integrated housing in their own town.

X

Morris Milgram is in his middle forties. He lives with his wife and two children in one of the earliest of his with Mr. Milgram on Monday night, that he was the main-integrated housing developments—Greenbelt Knoll. The "Johnny Appleseed" of integrated housing, who has spoken on his favorite subject in over fifty cities, does not sound much like a man with a social mission when interviewed on home ground. He sounds like an enthusiastic builder, with emphasis on the building.

And no wonder, when one sees what Milgram has built at Greenbelt Knoll. The site, just inside the western city limits of Philadelphia, is completely wooded and surrounded by park on four sides, including a two-acre private park for Greenbelt Knoll home-owners. There are nineteen award-winning homes in the $20,000 to $45,000 range. As the builder conducts his visitors on a tour of the project, he waxes eloquent over the skill and artistry employed to exploit every rise, every slope, every tree of the beautiful site and rolling terrain for the greater glory and loveliness of each individual home. His "pitch" spills over with attacks on the architects and builders who level off hills and cut down trees to make building simpler—and more uniformly ugly. He extolls the builders, like himself, who submit to the loveliness of nature instead of trying to obliterate it. He talks about drainage, flexibility of design, resale values.

Morris Milgram is a builder. But Morris Milgram is

also a man with a mission. He became a builder because his father-in-law, William M. Smelo, was a builder. Before Milgram joined Smelo's firm, Milgram told him, "Dad, I don't want to build homes that my friends can't live in, and some of my friends are Negroes."

The father-in-law believed in first things first. "Learn the business first, and then you can do what you want," he told his son-in-law. And Milgram "learned the business." For almost five years he worked on houses that would be sold only to whites, and then he announced he was ready, ready to build houses he could sell to all his friends, not just some. The first project, begun just before Greenbelt Knoll, was Concord Park Homes, the country's first planned open-occupancy development of private single homes. It consists of 139 three-and four-bedroom homes priced at $12,000 to $16,000—this was from 1954 to 1957—near the Philadelphia interchange of the Pennsylvania Turnpike, only a few miles from Greenbelt Knoll.

Milgram received encouragement and active support from many Quakers, particularly from George E. Otto, a leading Bucks County builder, who is now executive vice-president of Modern Community Developers. Today the board of directors and national advisory committee of MCD reads like a miniature Who's Who of American business, industrial, political and intellectual life. They include Dean Chamberlin, Albert S. Coolidge, Jackie Robinson, Gordon W. Allport, Stringfellow Barr, U. S. Senator Joseph S. Clark, Jr., Secretary of Agriculture Orville Freeman, the late Oscar Hammerstein, II, U. S. Senator Jacob K. Javits, Martin Luther King, Jr., American U. N. Delegate Philip Klutznick, Clarence Pickett, Bishop James A. Pike, A. Philip Randolph, Eleanor Roosevelt, Norman Thomas, U. S. Housing Administrator Robert C. Weaver, NAACP Executive Director Roy Wilkins.

Despite the encouragement and moral support, and some financial backing, the early days of Milgram's interracial housing developments were difficult. He would admit that things are equally difficult today but he would explain that the problems are less complex. When he started, he had all the problems of prejudice and resistance to living next door to Negroes, as well as the fears of Negroes about moving into a potentially hostile atmosphere. But he had other problems. He had to find and train personnel that would be not only sympathetic to his objectives but able to cope with the many delicate and some not so delicate aspects of integrated single-dwelling housing projects. He had to find investors who were willing to accept his thesis that interracial housing could be built by private entrepreneurs and produce a reasonable profit. He had to work out a formula for maintaining the projects on a truly interracial basis to answer the critics who insisted that within a few years the developments would be "all black."

Milgram solved his problems, sufficiently at least to put up the two Philadelphia developments and two more in Princeton, New Jersey, and to launch Modern Community Developers into new enterprises in several other states, among them Illinois.

From 1937 to 1947 Milgram had been employed by the Workers Defense League. This fact was to prove welcome ammunition for the opponents and a source of embarrassment to a few of the supporters of integrated housing in Deerfield. The familiar cry of "Red!" would be heard when Milgram's name was mentioned. For some the issue —at least in public—would not be interracial housing in Deerfield, but "Communist domination." And Supporters of the Floral Park project would find themselves arguing Milgram with their opponents, and not what Milgram was trying to do in Floral Park. More than one loyal "integrationist" expressed the private view that their row would be much easier to hoe if Milgram had been less politically controversial.

The issue of Milgram's politics was raised in the court

trial, although not—presumably—as a political issue. Milgram had been under cross-examination by the same Christensen who had earlier tried to get Pastor Berggren to label Milgram the prime mover in the "scheme . . . to impose racial restrictions . . ." upon Deerfield. After eliciting from Milgram the information about his employment with the Workers Defense League, the attorney for the defendants asked:

And where does the Workers Defense League get its money from?

A. It gets its money from contributions from the labor movement and from individuals.

Q. And it is the action arm of the Socialist Party, is it not?

A. No, it is not. It is a non-political agency formed in 1936 to prevent the Communists from capturing every labor and civil rights and minority rights case.

Q. All right, I am not—

A. It is backed by AFL-CIO unions, and by independents concerned with opposing the role of totalitarians of both the right and the left.

Q. And in what labor relations work did you engage during those eight—approximately eight years?

A. Our work consisted in helping sharecroppers, members of the Southern Tenants Farmers Union, later known as the National Farm Labor Union, of which we are the official defense agency, of defending workers arrested because they refused to work at substandard wages and of helping trade unions in their right to organize.

The Court: We are getting far afield, Counsel, from the issue.

Mr. Christensen: I think not, your Honor. I think this is a fraudulent statement in the prospectus [of Modern Community Developers]. He has represented himself as having engaged in labor relations, and if this examination is permitted to continue I will show that this is not labor relations work in any normal sense of that term. . . .

The Court: Then you are limiting your questions to the credibility of the witness. . . .

Mr. Christensen: To the credibility of the witness and the fraud in the representations in the stock prospectus.

The Court: It is a little far-reaching, but proceed. . . .

Mr. Christensen now introduced a variation on the same theme.

Q. Do you recall making a speech for the War Resisters League in 1942?

A. I might well have, sir.

Q. Well, you recall, do you not, that in late October of 1942 our troops were being attacked in Guadalcanal?

A. Yes.

Mr. Hunt: Your Honor, we object to this. This is going far afield. If he wants to—

The Court: I think it is. I don't—

Mr. Christensen: I want to show this man talks about civil rights but recognizes no civil obligations.

Mr. Hunt: Your Honor, we object to any such statement being made in the open court by this counsel. He has talked about fraud. . . . There are many officers and agents of MCD and Progress Development Corporation. If we go into this, then I suppose we will have to show who these other people are, how many of them served overseas in the war, how many were in the war effort, how many were Republicans, how many were Democrats . . .

The Court: I think it is going far afield, but he says he is going into it for the credibility of the witness. I feel I will have to let him go into it. I think it is immaterial, but go ahead.

Mr. Christensen: I will ask one more question, then. [To Milgram] On November 1, 1942, you were a speaker in Washington for the War Resisters League and you spoke on pacifism and freedom from tyranny, didn't you?

A. I must confess I don't recall the meeting, but I assume that I did.

Q. Have you given so many speeches on pacifism and on the rights of conscientious objectors you can't recall them all?

A. No, that is not it. I have given many speeches to many groups—

The Court: Counsel, if that is what it is going to, I don't see that it is related to the matter. . . . I think you have gone far enough on that question. . . . What his views are, I don't think we need go into that. The questions and answers concerning his views, concerning his activities on pacifism, may be stricken as no part of the case.

It is to be presumed that Judge Perry, in arriving at his decision, struck from the record the testimony on Milgram's political views and activities. Not so the residents of Deerfield, nor the leaders emerging to oppose Milgram. The Johnny Appleseed of integrated housing? A threat to the American way of life! Or at least to the Deerfield way of life.

XI

There were a few, very few, on November 19, who were angry about the reception given to the ministers, particularly to Berggren and Wykle, at the Village Board meeting the night before. One of them was John Lemmon, a life-long resident of the Deerfield area. "I approve of this whole plan," he told the reporter of the *Chicago Sun-Times* which carried his statement on Monday, November 23. "It is a fine thing. The builders are on strong legal and moral ground. Their subdivision will be a fine thing for the village. I'm one of the Deerfield residents who has everything he owns wrapped up in his house. Everybody worries about the economic aspects of this thing. The talk makes me wonder if we shouldn't open the banks instead of the churches in Deerfield on Sunday mornings."

Another resident who was disturbed by the jeers and angry disapproval which greeted the pleas of the ministers for Christian behavior was Adrien Ringuette, in whose home the builders and the village officials had met to discuss the Floral Park development. Ringuette was beginning to think in terms of organization, of rallying reasonable people to stem the growing tide of panic and anger. He spoke to John Lemmon and others and met with a sympathetic response, but the situation was too unclear to lend itself to any organized effort. Besides, there was no visible villain to attack, there was no specific action to oppose, no official position to contest, no definition of the issue—not yet.

XII

The stage was being set for the testing of Deerfield. There was a full weekend for talking and thinking and feeling. And the avidly read newspapers provided material.

On Friday, November 20, the *Chicago Sun-Times* carried the appeal of six Deerfield clergymen for acceptance of the integrated housing devlopment. Five ministers joined in a single statement in which each summarized the stand taken nationally by his church on racial discrimination. They were the Rev. Paul V. Berggren, Zion Lutheran Church; the Rev. Jack D. Parker, St. Gregory Episcopal Church; the Rev. Eugene M. Wykle, Bethlehem United Brethren Church; the Rev. Alfred S. Nickless, interim minister of the First Presbyterian Church, and the Rev. Russell R. Bletzer, North Shore Unitarian Church. The Rev. John J. O'Mara, pastor of Deerfield's only Roman

Catholic church, Holy Cross, commented in a separate statement: "This is an issue which should be decided on the principle of Christian justice."

The *Chicago Sun-Times* story of Friday did not carry each of the individual statements of the pastors but reported that the statements "amounted to a blanket appeal to church members for acceptance of Deerfield's proposed new integrated housing development." The Saturday *Chicago Sun-Times* carried an amplification of Father Parker's statement at the minister's request. This was the comment which he had omitted from his statement published Friday: "However, in this local situation we do not endorse the builder [of the subdivision] or his methods. We feel that they [the methods] are productive of the very feelings of ill will that he says he is seeking to combat." Later Friday, the paper reports, Father Parker added this further thought: "Negroes of the Episcopal faith who come to Deerfield will receive the same welcome as any other person."

On Saturday also, the *Daily News* carried an eight-column story by its popular religious editor, Dave Meade, giving the history of Progress Development Corporation and how it came to Deerfield. "The idea was hatched," wrote Meade,

by a group of Chicago area citizens, stimulated and encouraged by the American Friends Service Committee, a Quaker organization. . . . The AFSC program known as "Housing Opportunities" has been in existence for six years. Its purpose: "By education and encouragement of individual action to make housing available to all people without discrimination." In the course of its educational activities, the committee came in contact with various individuals who were interested in starting an interracial housing development or subdivision here. After bringing them together three or four years ago, the AFSC worked

closely with the orgnization, which formed a development group known as Lincoln Acres . . . . While studying
similar developments in other parts of the country, the
local group learned of the work of Modern Community
Developers of Princeton, N. J. . . . [who] had successfully
built two integrated projects in the Philadelphia area
and two in Princeton. As a result of meetings with
Morris Milgram, president of Modern Community Developers, and discussions that followed, the Chicago group
reorganized and became a subsidiary of the nationwide
firm based in Princeton. The subsidiary, Progress Development Corporation, was thus able to get the resources
and experience necessary to move ahead with the Deerfield project.

Most of the information in Meade's article was based
on information provided by Kale Williams, executive secretary of the Chicago regional office of the American Friends
Service Committee. The article went on to quote Williams
as saying that the AFSC, while not officially connected
with the project, had now become active in its behalf
through an educational campaign. "According to a study
now being published by the Fund for the Republic,"
Meade quoted Williams, "property values generally have
not declined in and around 75 privately built integrated
housing developments that were surveyed."

On Monday, November 23, the *Daily News* carried an
editorial which must have shaken those Deerfield readers
who had found comfort in attacking the Floral Park development on the basis of the builders' methods while
proclaiming their support of democratic principles including integration. The editorial was captioned "Meeting
a Test" and began with a story in which Mike was explaining socialism to Pat.

"It means," said Mike, "that if I had two million

dollars I'd give you one million, or if I had two houses I'd give you one."

"I see," replied Pat. "And suppose you had two pigs?"

"You go to blazes," said Mike. "You know I've got two pigs."

The editorial briefly describes the proposed Deerfield project and then goes on:

> Many residents of the North Shore suburb immediately registered strong opposition.
>
> The chances are good, it seems to us, that many of these protesters were reading the news from Little Rock in recent years with contempt for the unwillingness of the white community there to acknowledge that Negroes were people with the same rights as themselves.
>
> But, like Mike's socialism, it is different when you have a cozy community that someone suggests you share.

XIII

By the time Bob Danning went to lunch from his office on Monday, November 23, he had listened to all the wisecracks, he had answered all the questions he could take about Deerfield's "race problem."

"Hey, Bob; did you hear the one about the three-time loser?" "It it true everybody's selling?" "How much do you expect to lose on the house?" "Do you expect any violence?"

In mid-morning there had been a telephone call from the New York office asking him to send in a report ten days earlier than he had expected. Bob derived small comfort from the reassurances of his colleague at the other end of the line, who seemed to know all about Deerfield. "Well, you'll be out of it soon. Another couple of months at the most, and you'll be here with us and out of all that mess. In the meantime, don't let it get you!"

"Another couple of months at the most . . ." It was probably true, and he would be out of it, and he could let his neighbors worry about what was right and what was wrong. But in the meantime—how much of a loss would he take on the house?

In the restaurant Bob and one of the men from his office had to wait for a table. In back of them was a party of four, one of them a Negro, and this party was called first by the head waiter. The Negro murmured "Excuse me," as he brushed past Bob in the crowded foyer. "Black bastard!" Bob said—in his mind. And was miserable the rest of the afternoon.

When Joe Robbins went to the store that same Monday, November 23, he was prepared for a day of questions and comments and ribbing about Deerfield—and he got it. Saturday had been rough, but today was worse. As a matter of fact, he was astonished how many people knew that he lived in Deerfield, for much of his business came from people off the street.

A salesman just in from Cleveland told him the three-time loser story. At least five customers repeated it during the day. Fred Bernstein who owned the shoe store next door, and was something of a "character," dropped in during the slow morning to chat. Fred lived in Highland Park, just east of Deerfield, and both belonged to the same B'nai B'rith lodge. Fred was a liberal. He liked to boast of having voted four times for Roosevelt. An ardent Stevenson supporter in the last two presidential elections, he was already active in the advance guard of "Nominate Stevenson in 1960" workers.

"I'm proud of you, Joe!" he announced before Joe had a chance to say good morning. "The whole country will be behind you—you'll see. Deerfield will be the North's answer to those bigots in Little Rock who point the finger at prejudice in the North. We'll show them that . . ."

"Look, Fred, I'm not doing anthing that you should be proud of," Joe interrupted. "I'm not fighting the Civil War! I'm not fighting any war. Some guy from Philadelphia is building those houses, not me. And he didn't ask me, and he didn't ask anybody. And if he did ask me, I'd tell him to leave me alone! And to top it all, he's a Jew. We haven't got enough trouble?"

Fred plunged to the attack. By the time a customer's entry broke it up a half-hour later, he had invoked Lincoln, Roosevelt, Stevenson, Moses and the Prophets, the Constitution of the United States, and the B'nai B'rith charter. He had reviewed the persecution of the Jews from the destruction of the Temple through the Hitler era and his son's rejection by an Eastern medical school. "The only difference between them and us is that the Negroes are more visible. Don't kid yourself, Joe—it could happen to you!" he was saying when the customer walked in.

Joe was reasonably patient with his customers that day, a little less patient with the few salesmen who dropped in. He answered questions about Deerfield with a shrug and "Who knows what's right?" But when he got home that night and his son Marvin greeted him with, "The Kerwins say they're gonna move. Are we gonna move too, Dad?" Joe was ready to explode and he did: "Mind your own business and leave me alone!"

On the morning of November 23, Frank Gilbert was driving to Milwaukee to meet a client. As he drove along he reflected on the conversations at his home during the past weekend. Many of his neighbors had dropped in, some of them just nodding acquaintances. It was a pleasant surprise for the Gilberts, for they were rather reserved and on visiting terms with only their old friends.

All the visitors had one thing in mind—Floral Park and its two unfinished model homes looming black against the horizon. They seemed to want Frank's opinion on the matter, to know what his stand would be. If Frank was a bit taken aback at this attention, Paula Gilbert was not. She took it for granted that people should turn to her husband for his views—she always did.

At exactly ten o'clock, Frank Gilbert turned on the car radio for the news. The commentator led off with Deerfield. Frank couldn't get over the amount of attention his town was getting on the radio and in the newspapers. He couldn't understand why the possible sale of a few houses to Negroes should be of concern to anybody but the people directly involved—the residents of Deerfield. He wasn't too sure that it was the business of anybody else. As a matter of fact, he wasn't too sure there was a real issue, or that there need be one, unless people got all excited, which would certainly happen if this outside agitation continued.

The radio commentator was reporting a rumor that a petition would be circulated in Deerfield to get the Floral Park and Pear Tree subdivisions condemned for park purposes. One of Frank's neighbors had mentioned this possibility, and Frank's reaction was that he would have to think about it. Now he was thinking about it. Both the Park Board and the School Board had tried during the past year to get bond issues passed. The referendums had been rejected, but it did indicate that the officials, at least, thought they needed more land for park purposes. And condemnation was the legal and therefore the right way to get such land. But was it the right way to stop the sale of a few houses to Negroes?

Frank Gilbert hadn't had a chance yet to discuss the situation with his pastor, the Reverend Mr. Berggren. But he had heard that the pastor had already expressed pretty strong views in support of the builders and their objectives. Frank couldn't understand this. It wasn't Pastor Berggren's position that bothered him as much as the fact that he already had one. It didn't seem proper for an important man like the pastor to make up his mind so fast on an issue of such importance to his flock. There were many things to be considered.

First there was the law, the rights of the various parties involved—the rights of the builders, of the buyers, of the people in Deerfield whose properties might be affected. The law had to be observed at all times, and not just in the letter. The law had to be observed in the spirit, in the spirit of God and His teachings. What was right from a Christian viewpoint?

Certainly people had a God given right to live where they wished, Negroes as well as others. But did people have a God given right to intrude themselves where they were not wanted? As he drove along, Frank tried to understand why people would even want to go where they were unwelcome. And he had to assume that Negroes would be unwelcome in Deerfield because of all the fuss and to-do being made by his fellow Deerfieldians at the mere possibility that they might have a few Negro neighbors.

Oh, well, whatever happened, the whole issue would be settled peacefully and amicably. These were decent, reasonable people, God fearing people, good Americans. They would do the right thing in the right way.

When Frank got home that evening, his wife gave him a message. There would be a meeting that evening at the Deerfield Grammar School. It had been arranged by Pastor Berggren and other Deerfield ministers to have the builders and the village trustees "sit down quietly and become acquainted," as Berggren put it, "and talk about the problems involved."

XIV

On Saturday, November 21, Village President Koss called the Reverend Mr. Berggren in response to the invitation of the ministers to get together with the builders on Monday evening, November 23. Mr. Koss indicated several items that he wanted the builders to discuss and insisted that these be written down in agenda form. Pastor Berggren undertook to prepare such an agenda and to have it sent to all the members of the Village Board late Sunday night.

The Monday night meeting of the Village Board, the builders and the clergy had been intended as a private affair. But news of the meeting leaked out, and the Board was advised to invite the townspeople, lest they become apprehensive or angry at the idea of their trustees meeting secretly with the builders.

There was an overflow crowd at the Deerfield Village Hall on November 23 when the builders met with the village trustees to explain their objectives and plans. The people who couldn't get into the hall stood in the corridors and cloakrooms. And all America was present, for the first time, as television cameramen and radio and newspaper reporters joined the audience to record and report Deerfield's response, a Northern community's response, to the idea of receiving Negroes in its midst.

Village President Koss opened the meeting by announcing that the session had been requested by the village clergy to "hear plans of the developers, nothing else." The audience, he said, and the village trustees were to ask no questions, offer no comments.

It was a futile plea. Someone in the audience shouted, "We're going to have a Ku Klux Klan here! This is an NAACP program, and we want to ask questions!" Before the evening was over, the nation knew that integrated housing was far from welcome in Deerfield, that living in the North gave no immunity to fear and hate when whites are asked to live side by side with blacks.

This is how the meeting was reported the next day by the *Waukegan News-Sun*:

John W. Hunt, a member of Adlai E. Stevenson's law firm, a vice-president, assistant secretary and counsel of the firm, explained that the firm building the houses—the Progress Development Corporation—was a subsidiary of Modern Community Developers, Inc., a nationwide company chartered in New Jersey.

Plans called for 51 homes on two almost adjacent sites totalling 22 acres. The homes would be in the $30,000 class with four bedrooms, 2½ baths, attached garages and basements. . . . According to Hunt, 10 or 12 homes would be sold to Negroes.

Hunt then introduced other members of the firm. They included Morris Milgram, president of Modern Community Developers; Mrs. Walter Johnson, wife of the chairman of the University of Chicago history department and a vice-president [of Progress Development Corporation]; William Hooper, builder of an Ohio integrated development and Max Weinrib, executive vice-president of Progress.

Weinrib told how the firm had selected Deerfield as a site for the development.

After the land was acquired, "we told one of the finest architects in the country that we wanted plans for homes that would be at least as good as what Deerfield had," Weinrib said.

There was mumbling from the audience and one man shouted, "Yeah, but how many families will there be to a home?"

Village Trustee Arno D. Wehle got up from his seat and went into the hall then to quiet the hecklers.

Weinrib continued that the firm was not interested in downgrading the community. There was more grumbling and shouts of "Not much!"

Weinrib added that 18 of the lots would be a half acre and the smallest would be 9,000 square feet.

Hunt took over and said, "There is one thing that people don't understand about this firm. This is a continuing enterprise. We have a continuing interest to maintain this development."

He then explained that clauses in the contracts of the original purchases will give the Progress company the first option to sell the property for the original owners for several years. He did not say how many years.

This was the way in which the firm would maintain "controlled occupancy," he said. "We want 100 per cent white people in Deerfield," a woman in the audience shouted.

Hunt had a three-page statement from various authorities stating the effect of integrated development on property values. When he quoted from the statement that "property values do not necessarily go down and in some cases they go up," when Negroes move in, he was answered with catcalls.

"Go into Chicago and live there," one man shouted.

Several accused Hunt of making a statement for the press.

Hunt answered, "If prices do drop, it's because too many people sell at once."

To this the audience in a chorus asked "Why?"

Hunt, visibly shaken by this time, stumbled over his words as he said the problem is not economical but psychological. "The thought of Negroes moving in causes panic. It then develops into a chain reaction and all prices drop. If enough people predict a price drop and act on it, the prices of homes will drop."

He then said that there were no problems in two other projects developed in New Jersey by the firm. "In fact they have invited us back."

A few residents grumbled, "Then why don't you go back?"

. . . At this point Village President Koss called a recess so the village board could meet privately for a few minutes on the matter.

For a few minutes after the board members left there was confusion in the room. Then a man, who later identified himself as Harold C. Lewis, Riverwoods Road, got the attention of the crowd and made an appeal for calm and sanity.

"It is extremely important that we remain calm but determined," he said. "There are ways we can protect ourselves legally. We must beware of the trap that is being set for us in the press. They are trying to set this up as a fight between the good—headed by the clergy—and (what they call) the bigots of Deerfield."

Lewis added that this problem is not a question of integration. "We are intelligent enough to know what is coming and we will have to accept it. But we want to wait for the natural expansion" [of the Negroes], he said.

Lewis warned that the community had to act in the situation in a way that would not bring on criticism. "We should act with dignity but determination so that the problem is solved in the American way. But above all we must be determined that if we have to fight the battle of the whole nation here, we will," he said.

Lewis was loudly applauded as he stepped back into the audience.

At this point the Rev. Mr. Berggren called for attention and asked if he, or another clergyman, could chairman the rest of the meeting until the village board returned.

He was shouted down with "no, no" and the crowd chanted for Lewis to act as chairman.

Then the announcement of the "residents only meeting" at the American Legion home across the street was made.

The board returned and told the audience a meeting would be held at 8 p.m. the following evening in the Deerfield Grammar School to hear the opposition to the development.

What the *Waukegan News-Sun* did not report was the distribution among a select few of a pamphlet by Elizabeth Dilling, entitled *Red Hand Over Deerfield*. An officer of the Deerfield Citizens Committee, a man who was to work actively against the Floral Park project, commented

when he was handed a copy, "We don't need that stuff
here."

XV

Bob Danning was not among those who jeered and
booed. He was silent throughout the meeting, and when
John Hunt talked about property values dropping only when
people panicked, he looked about him and asked himself
whether angry people panic. "That's when you make your
money, eh?" his neighbor had shouted in reply to Hunt,
and Bob had edged away. He was glad that Helen hadn't
come to the meeting. In an almost disinterested way, he
reflected that she wouldn't think Deerfield was such a nice
town if she could see her neighbors in action. He watched
the TV men shifting their cameras to get different shots
of the hall and wondered if any of the people in his
national office in New York were watching, whether his
own face would show up on the screen to someone who
knew him. When Harold Lewis spoke, he listened at-
tentively, and as Lewis continued to speak, he listened
with hope. This was his kind of man—reasonable, calling
for reasoned action, above all calling for action. This was
no bigot. "Integration is coming," Lewis was saying. "You
can't avoid it. And when it is a natural situation . . .
we will accept it like constitutional people. But when the
approach is one of stealth and subterfuge, I don't believe
it's in the interest of integration, the community or the
Negro himself." Bob had joined in the vigorous applause
that greeted this statement. And when the meeting was
announced, the meeting to be held across the street and
closed to "foreigners and reporters," he joined his fellow
citizens of Deerfield who went there to accept the leadership of the man with a program, the reasonable man of
action—Harold Lewis.

Joe Robbins hadn't wanted Ethel to come to the meeting with him, but she had insisted. If there was a threat to her dream house, she wanted to know what it was. By the time John Hunt was finished talking, she was scared. When a man in back of her shouted "Throw them out!" as Max Weinrib was trying to speak, she begged Joe to take her home. But Joe wanted to stay, though he was as fearful as his wife. He wanted to know whether any program of action would emerge from the meeting. He too applauded loudly when Lewis made his "Integration is coming" speech, but he and Ethel didn't join the others who went over to the American Legion home, the meeting for residents only. His fear had come from the feeling of violence all around him, violence barely held in leash. And he wasn't sure he felt like a resident. On the way home, Ethel said to him, "Those people—the meeting—it felt like a lynch mob, like you see in Westerns."

"Yeh," replied Joe. "Like on TV."

"I'm glad you didn't go across the street, Joe. You won't go tomorrow night, will you?" she queried.

"I'll see," he answered. "But this I know: you are staying home tomorrow night. Maybe you can watch it on television!"

For Frank Gilbert the meeting was a shock from beginning to end. When it broke up to reconvene across the street, he did not join the friends and neighbors who urged him to come along. As he left the Village Hall to walk to his car, he went out of his way to avoid meeting and speaking with his pastor, the Reverend Mr. Berggren. He was ashamed. How could he apologize for the manner in which these people, his fellow citizens, many of them his fellow congregants, had received a spiritual leader of the community, and his own minister! He knew he should have risen to the aid of Pastor Berggren when he was hooted down in his attempt to bring order to the meeting. But he had been too shocked to move from his chair, let alone speak. When Paula had told him about the meeting earlier that evening, he had approved, and he was proud that it was his pastor who had taken the lead in bring-inging the builders and the village officials together. This was how reasonable people should behave: sit down together, talk, let people hear both sides of the question, go home and think about it. But these people, this mob! Were these the "reasonable, responsible citizens" about whom he had reassured his wife when she asked if there would be trouble? And this man Lewis—why, he didn't even live in Deerfield, not really. And this man, this stranger, was taking over the leadership of his community. Where were the trustees? Why had they refused to take a position, or at least to counsel their people? Why had they abdicated the leadership of Deerfield?

XVI

Harold C. Lewis is not yet forty years of age, but he has done well in the best American tradition. He lives close to Deerfield in an area known as Riverwoods. His home is a big ranch house on an extensive lot adjoining a natural forest. He maintains a large kennel of dogs. Executive vice-president of a Chicago brokerage firm, Lewis has the assured manner which inspires confidence. He speaks easily and well, and gives the impression of great poise.

The man who was the public symbol and active leader of the forces opposing integration in Deerfield has very little record of civic activity. He had opposed the establishment of a forest preserve near his home, and his opponents claimed it was because he was afraid that Negroes from neighboring Cook County would use it. Lewis comes from Indianapolis and his parents still live there, in a neighborhood now almost entirely occupied by Negroes. His background is Methodist.

Lewis has little use for some of the new "pseudo-scientific" trappings of modern community living— psychoanalysis and motivation studies and community planning. He deplores the growing role of government in private life, and the emphasis on the group rather than the individual. All of this he states fluently and with eloquence whether in the intimacy of a small group or from the public platform he came to occupy with increasing frequency as his role of leader became stronger.

This leadership role of Lewis would seem to be one of those fortuitous events when the right man happened to be in the right place at the right time. He may have had some contact with village officials in the two or three days preceding the November 23 meeting. He testified that he met Park Commissioner Donald Keller at a meeting in a private home the day before. But certainly he had no history of deep involvement in the affairs of Deerfield before the night of the Village Board meeting where Deerfield citizens had responded with enthusiastic cheers to his call for "legal and constitutional action" to thwart the "totalitarian scheme which was being forced down the people's throat."

The attorneys for the builders would subsequently try to prove that Lewis "conspired" with park and other village officials and individuals to "thwart" the builders. Lewis denied this both privately and in the courtroom. He testified that he did not meet Park Board President James Mitchell until December 3, and that the meeting took place at the home of one John Jursich. As for Jursich, Lewis did not meet him until the night of the meeting, November 23, and he couldn't recall who introduced them. One of the park commissioners, Dudley Dewey, he claimed never to have met, and another, Edward Walchli, he met for the first time on the evening of December 7, at Ethridge's Restaurant in Deerfield, a meeting which was adjourned to the home of John Jursich.

John Jursich, was to be a busy host between November 23 and December 7. Attorney Hunt did not doubt that the meetings in the Jursich home were the planning sessions of "conspirators." According to the testimony of the defendants (Jursich was not one of them), the meetings were informal affairs at which the subject of integration was never raised and where they indulged in "general conversation." In any event, Jursich, according to the testimony of Lewis, served as an informal contact person with Mitchell and other members of the Park Board, because Jursich knew them and Lewis did not.

Harold Lewis probably knew and was known by very few people in Deerfield before the meeting on November 23. But as he walked across the street from the Village Board meeting to the American Legion Hall, he was walking into the limelight of leadership, leadership that would earn him the scorn of some, the gratitude of many, the indifference of none.

XVII

There had been an overflow crowd at the Village Board meeting, but the meeting immediately after in the American Legion Hall was even more crowded. It was chaired by J. Robert York, president of the Library Board and an active member of his church. He opened the meeting with a plea that all sides of the issue be heard. At this, some of the people pointed to a small cluster of Floral Park supporters and began to heckle and jeer. "Come on. Tell us your side. Tell us why you want to wreck this community. Tell us why you want niggers here."

The hecklers focussed their attention on one woman

and insisted that she speak, but the woman refused. Someone called attention to a man with a camera, a photographer for *Life* magazine who happened to be a resident
of Deerfield. There were shouts of "Throw him out!" but
cooler heads prevailed. "They [presumably the pro-integra-
tionists] want us to do something rash. Let's not give
them the satisfaction." The photographer stayed. But the
tumult continued until somebody told the woman who
was leading the heckling to "shut up and get on with the
meeting."

If Harold Lewis wanted a citizens' committee to work
out a program of action, he certainly had a large and
cooperative group at the Legion Hall meeting. He made
another speech, repeating most of what he had said only
a short time before at the Village Board meeting, and again
the response was loudly approving.

Someone made a long speech on parks. Then someone
else, an attorney, urged that the park solution be followed
up. It was true, he said, that the last two or three park
referendums had been defeated, but by this time there
was possibly a change of sentiment. Perhaps, he continued, they were trying to avoid their social responsibilities, and this involves a "terrific price," but he was sure
everyone was willing to pay that price. "Let's add $10 to
the tax bill," he urged. "I'm for parks!"

The North Shore Residents Association grew out of
the meeting that night in the American Legion Hall, and
Harold Lewis became its president. But first a ten-man
committee of attorneys was named, chaired by Lewis, who
explained to reporters that this committee would present a
plan to the Village Board and residents at the meeting to
be held the following night at the Deerfield Grammar
School. "If we are given an affirmative vote by those there,
our first step will probably be to poll all the residents
of Deerfield to see how they stand on the project. Then we

will raise funds to take action." This is the statement Deerfield residents read in the *Waukegan News-Sun* the next day, November 24, as they prepared for the meeting that evening.

The *Waukegan News-Sun* story gave Lewis' interpretation of his "mandate" from the residents who attended the Legion Hall meeting. The obvious conclusion to be drawn, said Lewis, is that the people there want to oppose the Floral Park development because "it is being forced upon us by self-appointed people who think integration is not moving fast enough naturally. . . . We feel responsible to other communities," he added, "to resist, to avoid a precedent that may be harmful later to other communities and to the Negro himself."

The village officials, explained Lewis, "are in a difficult position. They cannot take the action they must take unless they have a clear and true mandate from the public." Thus, he said, his committee would not usurp the prerogatives of the village officials but would act in an advisory capacity.

Bob Danning was happy for the first time since that Tuesday, thirteen days ago, when he learned about the integrated housing development intended for Floral Park. It was after midnight when he got home from the Legion Hall, and Helen was still up, trembling with anxiety and tension. "What happened, Bob? I've been worried sick! I've heard so many stories!" she cried as he came into the living room. "Don't worry about a thing, dear," he replied jubilantly. "They have a committee, they have a program, and they have a terrific chairman. You'll hear all about it tomorrow night at the grammar school, because we're both going to be at that meeting. So first thing tomorrow morning you get a babysitter. We're going to stop those people!"

Helen didn't ask who "those people" were or how they were going to be stopped. The important thing was that Bob was happy again, which meant he wasn't worrying about losing money on the house, which in turn meant he thought his promotion was coming through soon and they would be moving East. Bob slept well that night, but Helen tossed and turned for hours before sleep came. Perhaps she didn't have to worry so much about money now, if Bob was right. Then why was she worried? Why did she feel just a little bit guilty?

Both Joe and Ethel Robbins had a bad night after the Village Board meeting, and Joe was exhausted and nervous and tense when he got up the next morning. "See if you can get a baby sitter for tonight," he told his wife before leaving for the store. "Maybe we'll take in a movie."

Frank Gilbert couldn't make up his mind about going to the meeting at the grammar school Tuesday night. He disliked big meetings anyway, and he knew that there would be an overflow crowd at the school. His wife had not asked him about the Village Board meeting, waiting—as usual—for him to volunteer the information. For reasons he himself did not understand, he told her nothing except that the pastor had been there, which she already knew.

The next day, when Frank read the newspapers—and that day he read them all—he decided that he would stay away from the meeting. In his mind he used the word "boycott." Lewis would head a ten-man committee of Deerfield attorneys to act as spokesman for the residents. Lewis would present a plan. Lewis said he was proud of the community and its people and they would work out a peaceful solution. Well, Frank Gilbert would not be party to government by default. Frank Gilbert would not associate himself with any effort or any persons that did not respect God's ministers. He was forced to admit, however, that some of the things Lewis had said were sensible—some of the things.

XVIII

When it had been announced that the builders would present their case to the village trustees on Monday evening, November 23, at least 150 people showed up.

When it had been announced that "residents only" would get together that same Monday night in the Legion Hall to discuss what could be done about Floral Park, some miracle of communication turned out more than 200 residents.

When it was anounced that on Tuesday, November 24, less than twenty-four hours later, there would be a meeting at the Deerfield Grammar School to hear the views of Deerfield residents on the subject of Floral Park, more than 600 turned out. They filled the 400 seats in the school gymnasium and spilled out into the corridors, into the streets, where a loudspeaker brought the proceedings to the crowd. There were some who even clung precariously to the ledges of the gymnasium windows.

The press was there—representatives of the Chicago and suburban papers, the national services, *Time* magazine.

The microphones and cameras of radio and television were there—from the local stations and the national networks.

The citizens of Deerfield had been asked by their elected leaders to speak their minds on integrated housing in their community. and they spoke.

For some the issue was property values, the threat to what was for most of them their biggest investment—their homes.

For some the issue was still the methods of the builders,

the "secrecy," the idea of having something "put over" on them.

But now there were new voices giving expression to old fears, old hates:

"Let in a few and they'll open the door to the rest."

"Black and white weren't meant to mix."

"I came here to get away from niggers, not to live with them."

There were other new voices in the school gym that night, far fewer voices but some of them just as angry. These were the voices that spoke about observing the "law of the land and the law of God," of fair play, of democracy.

Vice President Joseph Koss presided and opened the meeting with an admonition to the crowd to "demonstrate what Deerfield is most noted for—democratic solutions to problems." Then trustee Arno Wehle read a statement in behalf of the Village Board, in which he urged calm. "Since we are on the front pages, let us bring credit to Deerfield."

This preoccupation with Deerfield's sudden projection into the spotlight of national attention was manifested again in the speech of Harold Lewis. He was the first in the long list of private citizens who responded to the Village Board's invitation to "present their views." First he explained the role of his committee of ten local lawyers as "fact-finding." The committee was entirely unofficial, he emphasized, and would advise and cooperate with the Village Board. "We feel we are compelled to take some such step because of the spotlight put on Deerfield."

Residents resented the manner in which integration was being brought to Deerfield, he said, and he wondered out loud if there had not been an "invasion of constitutional rights of the population of Deerfield." Citizens "should avoid discussing integration because that issue has been settled; we cannot fight integration." But the citizens of

Deerfield could fight the "improper approach," and could fight it with every hope of success.

Lewis then announced that his committee would immediately undertake a written poll of residents "to ascertain how many are FOR and how many are AGAINST the integration project." From this poll the committee would determine the "real feeling" of the community. From those who indicated opposition to the integration scheme, funds would be asked to finance a court fight or whatever other measures would be undertaken.

The committee would keep the community informed as to its progress, said Lewis, through publications and meetings, and would also combat unfounded rumors. He asked for volunteers from the audience to help conduct the poll. (His committee later announced that more than 200 residents responded to the call.)

During the course of his speech, which was interrupted frequently by loud applause and cheers, Lewis made his own plea for calm. He cautioned residents not to sell their homes just because of the integration issue. "I have seen no evidence of panic, although the other side seems to be talking about it all the time." And he added, "There won't be much of a market for homes in Deerfield anyway until this issue is settled. . . . We have an obligation to the nation to fight this project—but not with bitterness and prejudice. . . . Let's be mindful of outside public reaction. Give thought to your remarks when asked for opinions."

And this closing plea: "Let's act like good Americans. If we win, we'll be happy; if we lose, let's be good sports."

There was wild applause and loud cheering. It was a bad moment for a woman, identifying herself as coming from Chicago, to get up and speak, for she spoke in favor of the integrated development and was hooted down. "This meeting is for residents only!" "We don't need outsiders telling us what to do!"

The next speaker was a resident. "I am greatly impressed

with Lewis' integrity, presentations, and outline of actions," he said. "I move that we leave the problems in the hands of Lewis and get some action!"

Again the audience gave loud approval. The opposition to these ideas was small, but it was courageously represented. The next speaker was Theodor Repsholdt, a history teacher at Highland Park High School where Deerfield children attend. He told the audience that he had just been assigned to teach at the new Deerfield High School. "Since I am teaching your children . . . you should know where I stand. I want to go on record in favor of the project."

"We don't want you teaching our children," one woman shouted. "Fire him!" a man shouted, and others took up the cry.

Repsholdt stood his ground. "Firing doesn't bother me," he replied. "Just as there is a shortage of housing, there is a shortage of teachers."

"Then resign! Why don't you resign?" the audience shouted back.

"If I could afford one of those 51 houses, I would buy it," was Repsholdt's answer.

John Lemmon and a few other hardy spirits urged acceptance of the project. It would be good for the community. It would be an example for the nation. It would give the lie to those nations that attacked the United States in the forum of world opinion for its discrimination against minorities. It was right, it was the Christian thing to do.

But the efforts of this small group went for naught that night. Their voices were lost among the jeers and boos. One of the village trustees told a reporter that he was disgusted with the spectacle. "The people are acting like a bunch of kindergarten children," he said. One of the residents was less charitable in his description of the mood of the meeting. "For the first time in my life," he said afterwards, "I knew what it felt like to be in a lynch mob. I had the feeling that if they could have fixed the blame on one person, they would have tarred and feathered him or strung him up!"

That resident was more fearful, perhaps, than the circumstances justified. Certainly the mood of the crowd was almost constantly angry, often ugly. One woman who began to speak in favor of integration collapsed in tears. Another woman who had wanted to speak in support of the project said afterwards, "I didn't get up because when I saw their faces, I was afraid."

After Repsholdt, Lemmon, and the few others had spoken or attempted to speak in favor of the Floral Park project, all those who followed made it clear that the project was not welcome in Deerfield. They brought forth a long list of complaints, fears and accusations.

One woman who said she was against the project, not against integration, announced that there was proof that certain persons affiliated with the builders were "connected with the Communist Party." (Elizabeth Dilling had held a meeting in Deerfield the night before and had distributed a pamphlet entitled *Red Hand Over Deerfield*. It could easily have been the source of this comment and many of those that followed.)

Another resident who proclaimed his support of the idea of integration accused the builders of practising discrimination by their controlled-occupancy policy. (A federal judge was to take a similar position about the builders a few months later.)

Another speaker accused the developers of hypocrisy in their talk about brotherhood. "By forcing this thing on us, they're creating more prejudice than brotherhood!"

One resident, a realtor, estimated for the audience that the drop in real estate values as a result of the integrated project could be $12,000,000. The developers, he said, had "stirred up a great hate that was not there before."

Several people described calls they had received offering them half the value of their homes or less. A resident who had once lived in Yellow Springs, Ohio, the site of another integrated development, said that property values there had dropped and that there was much tension, and white people had begun to move away. (At the Village Hall meeting the previous night, William Hooper, the builder of that Yellow Springs development and a member of the Progress board of directors, had cited the same development as an example of how integrated housing worked successfully.)

"I don't think anyone who would want to be a part of Deerfield would move into these houses."

"We weren't consulted to see if we want to be a part of this experiment."

"How will Negro occupancy be controlled? How do we know this project won't expand into other sections of town?"

"If the people who are pushing this project have any religion in their souls, how can they go before God knowing they have stirred up hatred in me and many of you, toward Negroes, that wasn't there before?"

When one woman picked up this last comment by saying, "God made all of us," another woman replied, "God also made the bluebird and the blackbird, but you don't see them in the same nest." To which the first woman answered, "They don't live in the same nest, but they do live in the same tree." Whereupon the second woman said, "I beg to differ. They just can't mix."

"The developers are trying to wreck the community."

"The Unitarians are behind this!"

"The Quakers are behind this!"

And in the same tone of accusation, "The ministers are behind this!"

This one was not shouted out, but muttered in the presence of a reporter: "We should never have let the Jews into Deerfield."

And finally, out loud for everyone to hear and without loud applause but with many nods of approval: "I happen to work with those people [Negroes], but I don't want to live with them. If I have to move further out to get away, so help me God, I will!"

After urging residents to speak their minds to any trustees they met, Village President Koss gaveled the meeting to a close.

XIX

Bob and Helen Danning were silent as they drove back from the meeting. When they arrived at the house, Helen went in to pay the baby sitter and Bob waited outside to drive her home. When Bob returned, Helen was in the kitchen drinking coffee. She poured a cup for him, and for a long time both sat there without speaking. Finally, Helen broke the silence.

"They will stop the project, won't they?" she asked, and her question was a statement.

"Yes," replied Bob. "I guess they will."

"Are you joining the committee?"

"I suppose so."

Helen said nothing. Bob waited a few moments and then asked, almost querulously, "Why shouldn't I join? I can't let other people do my dirty work for me."

"That's just what I mean," she said. "The whole thing is such a mess, and I don't see why you have to get mixed up in it. It's not really our town. We'll be out of here soon, maybe in two or three months you told me. Why get involved now?" And her tone was pleading.

"We have lived here for a few years," Bob answered slowly. "Those people at the meeting tonight are our friends, some of them. And all of them are our neighbors. We just can't walk out on them."

"But I thought all you cared about was to get our money out of the house when the time comes to sell it."

Now Bob was hurt. "That's not fair, Helen. Sure, I was worried about the money, and maybe I still am—a little bit. But now I honestly don't think there will be a panic, and I think the prices will hold up. Maybe we won't get the thirty or thirty-one thousand we talked about, but I'm sure we'll get what we put into it. We won't lose anything."

Bob paused a moment, and then went on as though explaining to himself. "It's just that I don't think it's right to make guinea pigs out of decent people who are getting along with each other and not bothering anybody. I just don't think it's right to force people. I just don't think it's right."

"But Bob, the awful things those people said!" Helen shook her head in disbelief of her own words. "I was stunned! They seem to be such nice people—like that woman who told that stupid story about God making the bluebirds and the blackbirds. And the way they went after that teacher, that Repsholdt man!"

Bob laughed. "Forgive me, dear," he said. "I don't mean to be rude, but I just remembered that on the way home from last night's meeting I was thinking to myself that you wouldn't be so proud of those 'nice' neighbors you're always talking about if you could see them as I did. And now you're saying it yourself!"

Then he became serious again. "Those people you're talking about are the ones who yell at every meeting, no matter what the issue is. You'll find them in every town. They're not exactly the lunatic fringe, but they're the ones who make a lot of noise. But the real people of this town, and I'm not being a snob, are the people like us. We're not bigots. We don't go around calling people names. And I don't think we want to deny Negroes or anybody else the right to decent homes, just as good as ours. But not next door. It just doesn't work."

"I'm getting more confused by the minute," Helen said. "Let's go to bed. I'll do the dishes in the morning."

As they went up the half-flight to their bedroom, Helen added, "I guess you feel it's your duty to join the committee," and her voice underscored the word duty.

"Yes," Bob answered. "I guess you could call it that."

As Helen was falling asleep, she tried to picture Susan bringing home a colored classmate for lunch. "Bob is right," she thought. "The same school, yes. But not next door."

Joe and Ethel Robbins read about the meeting in Wednesday's newspapers. Joe had one of the Chicago papers in front of him when his friend Fred Bernstein came into the store. Fred didn't badger Joe about Deerfield this time as he had been doing for several days. Joe was obviously upset and unhappy. "Were you there?" he asked him.

"No," Joe answered. "Ethel and I went to the movies. One meeting was enough for me."

Fred patted him sympathetically on the shoulder, and went back to his own store. When Joe got home that night, it was clear that Ethel was bursting with the need to talk, to give vent to emotions that had been churning within her all day. But she waited until dinner was finished, the dishes done and the children in bed, before she confronted her husband.

"I want to get out of here, Joe," she announced. "The newspapers, the radio, the way the neighbors are talking. You should have heard Nan Kerwin! Any minute I expected her to get a rope and go after that school teacher! And what she said about that minister, the one from the Lutheran church, that Berwin . . ."

"Berggren," Joe corrected her.

"Berggren," she repeated. "Isn't it her own minister? And in the First National this morning, I thought . . ."

Joe grabbed her by the shoulders and shook her gently. "Stop it, Ethel!" he said. "You're getting hysterical. A few people get excited and you fly off the handle. You're not in Mississippi. This is Deerfield, this is Illinois. These people don't go around lynching anybody. They're worried about this new project, that's all. So they let off a little steam."

But Ethel would not be stopped.

"I don't care where we are," she cried, "as long as it's not here. You should hear the children. Marvin came running in after school yelling, 'Niggers are moving here! And we're going to get rid of 'em!' I was so shocked I slapped his face. Can you imagine? I slapped Marvin in the face! I made him cry. And later I found out the poor kid didn't even know what he was saying. He heard Ted Kerwin and some of the older boys yelling it in some game they were playing, so he yelled it too. What's going to happen to the children, Joe? The next thing you know they'll be yelling 'dirty Jew' at them. Please, Joe, let's get out. I don't care if we lose money on the house, but at least we won't be afraid."

Joe attempted to calm his wife who was now in tears. "Look, Ethel," he said, "you know you get easily excited. But honestly, there's nothing to worry about. A bunch of kids start yelling names they don't even understand. You have to remember they're kids. Have you forgotten we did the same thing when we were kids on the West Side? There are responsible people in this town, and they'll know what to do. And the busybodies like Nan Kerwin and the people who made all that uproar last night, you find them everywhere. We're going to stay put, for now anyway." A note of anger was edging into Joe's voice. "We're not moving," he said. "I don't care if they move in next door! They aren't going to push us out!"

When she thought later about what Joe had said, Ethel wasn't sure that Joe had meant Negroes when he said, "They aren't going to push us out." Joe didn't know, either.

Frank Gilbert had read about the meeting in the newspapers and had received a blow-by-blow description from fellow commuters on the train the next morning. He was telling his wife about it at dinner that evening.

"I just don't understand what has happened to this town! Here is a man like Tom Jenkins, a responsible citizen, goes to his church every Sunday—at least that's what I always thought, and you would say that he's a reasonable, thinking man. And he has the nerve to ask me if I'm going to join that committee of theirs, that thing that Lewis is organizing!"

Louise burst in excitedly. "A lot of the kids at the high school say their dads are going to join. And are they ever mad at Mr. Repsholdt!"

Frank turned slowly to his daughter. "Who is mad at Mr. Repsholdt—your classmates or their fathers?"

"Oh, no, Dad!" Louise answered. "Not the kids. The fathers. They say he has no right to teach kids. Karen said her father called him a 'nigger-lover.' "

Paula Gilbert turned pale. "Don't you ever say things like that again, Louise, do you hear?" she exclaimed.

But Frank was even more pale, and his voice was tense with emotion as he addressed his daughter.

"You listen carefully, Louise. You tell those friends of yours in school that Mr. Repsholdt is a God fearing Lutheran, a decent upstanding Christian. You can tell them that your father is not going to join any committee to take over responsibilities that belong to the properly constituted authorities of this town. And you tell them your dad would rather have a fine intelligent Negro living next door to him than some of their fathers!"

Louise Gilbert and her mother were struck dumb. They

71

had never heard Frank Gilbert speak with such violence.

The meal was finished in silence, and after dinner Frank retired to his study. As Louise was helping with the dishes in the kitchen, she asked her mother, "Why is Dad so mad? Is it because Mr. Repsholdt is a Lutheran like us?"

"I don't think so, dear," Mrs. Gilbert replied. "Your father has principles," and now there was pride in her voice, "and he thinks everybody has principles, or should have. Your father sticks to his principles."

Louise wasn't too sure her question had been answered, but she said nothing more. Her mother, however, had another thought to add. "You don't really have to tell your friends all those things your father said," and Mrs. Gilbert lowered her voice as she spoke. "I mean it wasn't as though he was insisting, at least not the way he said it. He was just a little excited."

Mrs. Gilbert didn't like trouble.

As she put away the dish towels she wondered what it would be like to have Negro neighbors. She had read somewhere that there were Negroes who were Lutherans.

XX

The meeting at the Deerfield Grammar School was the last of the large public meetings held for the purpose of "hearing the views of the residents." The struggle over the Floral Park development now entered a new phase, the phase of organization. Now the time had come for drawing the lines of battle, for recruiting adherents.

The immediate terrain of battle was the poll of the villagers announced by the Lewis committee. The weapons would be leaflets, paid advertisements in the *Deerfield Review*, meetings, door-to-door visits.

Until now the residents of Deerfield had had few individuals on whom to focus their anger and indignation—on either side. For those who opposed the project the enemy was Milgram, Weinrib, the Chicago newspapers. But these were not private citizens, neighbors. Being angry at them was an almost impersonal thing. Nor were the ministers, with their varying degrees of active support for the project, proper objects of real resentment, with the possible exception of Berggren. No one really expected a "man of God" to come out *against* integration. Rippey, Repsholdt, Ringuette, Lemmon—they were different. As the leaders of the Citizens for Human Rights they were visible targets, they were residents of Deerfield who had betrayed their friends and neighbors. And the list would grow longer as Deerfield mobilized for the bitter struggle.

The leaders of the Human Rights group received threatening letters and telephone calls—all anonymous. Rippey was asked to choose between his law firm and his place on the board of directors of Progress Development Corporation. Although there was no evidence of pressure on the part of his school board to make Repsholdt resign his post, many private citizens made it clear to the young teacher that they would be happier to see him in another job. Ringuette, an attorney, did not have to worry about his job, but his assumption of the chairmanship of the Human Rights committee made him a special target for the anonymous telephone calls and letters and the general hostility of many of his neighbors.

The most conspicuous target for the anti-Floral Park forces, however, was John Lemmon. It was easy to be against Lemmon because he already had something of a reputation for being "different," an "odd-ball." In his late thirties, he is married and has five children, and lives in a two-story house in the old part of the village. This house became the subject of considerable rumor and speculation because of a series of unexplained fires that broke out in it during and after the heat of the integrated housing issue.

John Lemmon's problems resulting from his role in the Deerfield housing struggle were not limited to his job. He is currently involved in a lawsuit against some of the village officials for circulating a purported news release in which Lemmon is described as addressing a left-wing students organization on the University of Michigan campus on May 1, 1960. The release is on the letterhead of CORE, the Chicago Committee on Racial Equality, and is dated May 2, 1960:

SAYS THIS COUNTRY IS NOT WORTH SAVING

Ann Arbor, Mich., May 1—Speaking before the national convention of the left-wing "Students For A Democratic Society" today, John E. Lemmon of Deerfield, Illinois, said, "It is no longer possible to work within the framework of the capitalistic police state that we refer to as the United States. The totalitarian methods used in this country today make impossible a peaceful revolution of the working class. . . . We must, all of us, go back to our campuses and homes and double our efforts to bring about a sovietized United States." Lemmon also said, "This country is far beyond the point where it might be worth saving." After a long tribute to the USSR, Lemmon was given a standing ovation. The "Students For a Democratic Society" before which Lemmon spoke has been cited by the Attorney General of the United States as "clearly subversive."

CORE publishes news release of this nature in an effort to point out that while we believe in racial equality for all, we do not approve or want the assistance of known subversives in this work. Racial equality is a problem that concerns all loyal Americans. We abhor and deny the right of subversives to exploit this problem in their efforts to spread discontent and provide propaganda for the enemies of the United States.

May 2, 1960

140 copies

CORE denied all knowledge of the release. As for Lemmon, he had attended a family dinner at the home of his mother-in-law in Western Springs, Illinois, and then returned to Deerfield where that night he attended a meeting of the Deerfield Citizens for Human Rights.

Lemmon was conspicuous—therefore logical to attack—because he had become the public spokesman of the integrationist forces. In fact, he appeared at so many meetings with Harold Lewis to debate the issue of interracial housing in Deerfield that at one point he suggested to his opponent that they become a team and "put the act on the road." But the man who could joke with his antagonist was a determined and hard fighter, determined and hard enough to make many enemies less tolerant and far more bitter than Lewis. In fact, it was to Lewis that a not untypical letter was addressed on the subject of Lemmon, with copies to Ringuette, Hunt, Mrs. Robert Pettis (then editor of the *Deerfield Review* and subsequently named as a defendant by Lemmon for passing out on some of the purported CORE news releases), and Lemmon himself. The letter reads:

Dear Mr. Lewis,

I take this opportunity to commend you on the stand that you have taken on the integration issue in Deerfield. There must be many people like myself that appreciate your efforts to protect our community. I am not in a position to publicly identify myself with your fight, but I have made a substantial contribution to the Deerfield Defense Fund.

As you are probably aware, Jack Lemmon is the real power behind the Deerfield Citizens for Human Rights. I have known this man for a number of years and am well aware of the danger he poses to our community. There are a number of things that you should know about Lemmon that will enable you to better fight him and his kind. Those of us who know this man, realize that he represents a great threat to our country and way of life. For many years he has been a Socialist. He is a very active members of the NAACP. He is an atheist. While he has not been named by any Congressional committee, he is most friendly with a number of individuals who have been named as Communist party members. At one time he was a subscriber to the *Daily Worker*. He has been active with a number of organizations that have been cited. The library in his home contains a number of books by Marx & Engels. These books he makes available to his friends and any young people he can get to read them. For many years he has espoused the theories of free love, atheism, socialism, communism and niggerism.

I firmly believe that this one man has done more to destroy our way of life in this area than any other individual or group. He goes quietly on his way undermining our government and the social fibre of our community. He should be stopped before it is too late. God only knows how many young people and children he has been able to pervert so that even now they are doing his ungodly work for him. Wake up Mr. Lewis and recognize who our enemy is. Point out to the people of Deerfield that this fiend is at work within our community.

With best wishes for your work and God bless you.

(No Signature)

John Lemmon was undoubtedly a political liberal, and he was supporting an interracial housing project involving another political liberal, Morris Milgram, and the admitted

Socialist Max Weinrib. And Lemmon's views on religion
were anything but conformist. But Lemmon was to share
with far less conspicuous and far more conservative neighbors aligned with him in the fight for integrated housing in Deerfield the labels of "atheist," "communist,"
"nigger-lover."

XXI

For the few—at present—who supported the integrated
project, their wrath had been focussed largely on Harold
Lewis and the village trustees. Father Parker's statements
had incurred the indignation of some, and there were those
who considered the neutrality of the *Deerfield Review* a
little too heavily weighted in favor of the anti–integration-
ists. But in terms of the across-the-back-fence relationships,
the camaraderie of the commuter trains, the neighborly
greetings and conversations in stores—the bitterness had
not yet begun to any noticeable degree, because the residents themselves had not yet begun to register their active
support of one side or the other.

The organization of the North Shore Residents Association and the Deerfield Citizens for Human Rights gave
the residents of Deerfield the opportunity to stand up and
be counted. In point of fact, comparatively few people
actually became members. But they made contributions to
the organization which represented their particular point
of view, and attended its meetings.

The North Shore Residents Association had really begun
the night of the "Residents Only" meeting at the American Legion Hall, with the appointment of ten lawyers to
work with Harold Lewis as a Citizens Committee. But the
formal announcement of a full-blown membership organization to fight the integrated project came on Sunday,
November 29. The announcement was carried in the Chi-

But Not Next Door

cago papers on Monday, and in the news columns of the *Deerfield Review* on Thursday. In addition to the news story, the *Deerfield Review* carried a full-page advertisement stating the aims of the North Shore Residents Association, and calling for contributions and volunteers. The advertisement closed with an editorial signed "Hal Lewis," and listed the officers and board as follows:

H. C. Lewis, chairman; H. H. Garbrecht, vice-chairman; H. A. Petit; R. D. Rierson; R. G. Mullen; Dr. L. Bronstein, treasurer; D. J. Maundrell; F. M. Blake. All were listed as residents of Deerfield, and all were to be named as defendants when the builders brought suit against Deerfield village officials and certain private citizens for "conspiring" to block the Floral Park project.

After explaining that the organization came into being in response to the expressed wishes of the people of Deerfield, the advertisement briefly states the history of the project and the reaction to its announcement in Deerfield.

This section of the advertisement closes with a summary of the public status of the issue. "Skilled public relations people working for the builders seem to have enlisted the facilities of certain newspapers, radio and television stations, in representing to the public, that favoring this integrated project are most religious leaders, humanitarians, and educators, and that opposing it are only the 'bigots' of Deerfield.

"The facts are that the overwhelming majority of people of Deerfield, including educators and clergy, are resolutely opposed to this project."

Then there follows a three-part section:

WE BELIEVE:

1. That every business institution has a moral and legal obligation to make full and complete disclosure to any municipality from which it seeks to obtain approval of

78

its plans or projects and any necessary licenses or permits. This is particularly mandatory when those plans or projects are of such a nature as to effect profound changes on the character, security, sociological aspect or economic well-being of that municipality.

2. That any such plans . . . imply an extraordinary responsibility upon the petitioner to make full and complete disclosure.

3. That deliberate concealment is an act of bad faith that breaches any and all contracts, agreements or covenants into which the municipality may have unwittingly entered.

WE REPUDIATE:

1. The totalitarian doctrine that the end justifies the means.

2. Self-appointed Master Planners who seek to impose their will upon helpless communities with complete disregard for the communities' right of self-expression.

3. The use of stealth, subterfuge, and deceit, wherever it may be found, and in whatever guise.

4. Claims of noble purpose where ignoble methods are employed for the purpose of profit.

5. "Panic Brokers" who seek to create problems where none formerly existed, who create and fan the flames of racial misunderstanding, who seek to capitalize on the turmoil inherent.

WE ACCEPT:

1. The principle of integration as it applies to normal and natural development—that arises from demonstrated need, or desire, and that emanates directly from the individual himself, regardless of race.

2. *We accept and will defend* every provision of the Constitution of the United States of America, including the NINTH AMENDMENT which reads, "*The enumeration in the constitution of certain rights shall not be construed to deny or disparage others retained by the people.*"

THAT IS OUR POSITION—ONLY THAT AND NOTHING MORE!

The advertisement announces that a house-to-house poll will get under way the following Thursday, urges contributions of money and help, and urges residents not to offer their homes for sale. Then follows the Lewis editorial.

Lewis repeats the attack on the newspapers and other communications media, saying, "In these days of rigged television shows and biased reporting, we are not surprised that some media sacrifice truth . . . for the sake of attracting greater audience or readership. Yet, why some of these media should distort reports simply to try to put the peaceful people of Deerfield in a bad light passes understanding."

Then follow a few kind words for "some" newspapers, presumably including the *Deerfield Review*, "that have some decent consideration for the 16,000 people of Deerfield who have built their fine community and respect for the old-fashioned virtues of honesty and truthfulness."

The figure of 16,000 used in the editorial, incidentally, probably includes some of the adjacent areas like Lewis' own village.

The editorial closes with an assertion of the moral character of the resistance to the Floral Park project. "The vast majority of the people of Deerfield," writes Lewis, "are certain that they are morally right in resisting this thing. And they are convinced a small group of outside developers, no matter how lofty their claimed objectives, cannot master legal technicalities to compel 16,000 Deerfield residents to submit to their dictates."

XXII

The announcement of the formation of the Deerfield Citizens for Human Rights was carried in the newspapers almost simultaneously with that of the North Shore Residents Association. On Wednesday, November 25, the day after the public meeting at the grammar school, several people met at the home of Jack Lemmon. It was agreed that Adrien Ringuette would set up an organization meeting on the following Sunday, and everyone present was to contact people who might be interested in participating.

There was another planning meeting in Ringuette's home on Friday, and on Sunday, November 29, at the home of magazine editor Wesley Wise, the organization meeting of the Deerfield Citizens for Human Rights was held. Some thirty to thirty-five people were present, and from this group a steering committee was selected. They included twelve lawyers, two businessmen, a magazine editor, a school teacher, and four housewives. For the moment no chairman was named, so that any abuse that fell upon the group might be shared by all. Daniel Walker, former president of the Democratic Federation of Illinois and a reported candidate for Attorney General nomination in the Democratic primary, explained the purposes of the new group as supporting the constitutional "rights of all citizens to purchase, sell and hold real and personal property."

"The Citizens' Committee feels," he said, "that the integration of minority groups in Deerfield can benefit the area. The committee will urge village officials to uphold the legal and moral right of all people who live in the suburbs. . . ." Walker emphasized that the group was in no way affiliated with any developer and builder.

The pressure, particularly from the press, for a spokesman became great and on Wednesday, December 2, the steering committee met and elected Adrien Ringuette temporary chairman; and Bernard Katz, also an attorney, vice-chairman. Other members of the committee were John Lemmon, Theodor Repsholdt, Mary Ellen Sabato, Daniel Walker, Wesley Wise, Alice Klyce, Charlotte Scotch, Sally Burns, and Cyril Fritz.

There were now seventy members of the Human Rights group, and on Thursday, they rented an office on Waukegan Road, in the business section of the village.

The North Shore Residents Association and the Deerfield Citizens for Human Rights would appear to have had much in common, while fighting on opposite sides of the issue which spawned them. Both groups were the spontaneous response to the expressed wishes of their partisans for action. Both disclaimed outside ties: the Human Rights group with the builders, the Residents Association with the Village Board and Park Board.

The two groups were in favor of integration, both were dedicated to fact-finding, both intended to scotch false rumors. They had one difference: the Human Rights group was FOR the Floral Park project, the Residents Association was AGAINST the Floral Park project.

As the two groups prepared for the first major test of strength, the poll of residents, they could count on certain forces, both internal and from the outside, to work in their behalf. The Human Rights committee had the support of most of the clergy, in some instances active support. The Chicago press was unanimously on their side, not only in the editorial columns, but in the supporting material they furnished in the way of news stories giving the background of the Deerfield situation and often slanted to give prominence to the views of proponents of the project; feature articles showing how well Modern Community Developers' projects had worked out elsewhere, how other interracial housing developments had been successful. Radio and TV programs by and large seemed to support the integration forces. On the Sunday after the public meeting there had been several local and national radio and TV programs. One of them was Chet Huntley's *Time: Present* on NBC-TV, which carried an interview with Milgram and pictures of two of his developments in the East; shots and tapes of some of the Village Board meetings and the big public meetings; and pictures of Father Parker shaking hands with his parishioners as they left St. Gregory Episcopal Church, in the shadow of the development on two sides of the church. (The *Deerfield Review* gave a full report on this program including a description of shots of "white and Negro women playing bridge and having parties together" in one of Milgram's developments.)

The North Shore Residents Association did not have the support of leadership like the clergy, and the village officials had proclaimed their neutrality and with only a few exceptions strove mightily to maintain that position, at least in public. One of those exceptions was Donald Keller, member of the Deerfield Park Board, who wrote a letter on Friday, November 27, to the *Deerfield Review* which was published in the issue appearing the following Thursday. The article which accompanied the letter said it was "typical of scores of other letters that have been pouring into the Village Hall and to the *Deerfield Review* during the past few days." Mr. Keller was a former president of PTA of the Wilmot School, for which the Park Board purportedly wanted land. The Wilmot School is adjacent to the controversial housing development.

Mr. Keller wrote, in part:

> There are those who would have the people of Deerfield think that this whole question is one of the entrance of one or more Negro families to our community. This is absolutely untrue. The folks who allude to this are as misguided as those who would incite racialism for racialism's sake. I feel certain that if a Negro family purchased a home and moved into the community of Deerfield— on their own—this would cause no more concern than the many other transients of any race or creed who move into and out of this village.

The letter went on to attack the builders for using Deerfield residents as "test tube guinea pigs" for their "little game of racial chess" and accused them of having set back the cause of racial good-will several hundreds of years. Keller asked the builders why they could not "take their plan and develop a new community from scratch" with

people "completely amenable to this new step in society."
He spoke of growing up in Philadelphia with Negroes and
what a pleasant association it was. The controlled-occupancy policy, he said, is discrimination in itself. "By what
super power are these people to decide which of the Negro
race are to become our neighbors?"

He concluded:

> If because you are against the enforcement of the will
> of the few on the many and if you are concerned about
> your own rights as a private citizen please do not be
> baited by the one remark you will hear from these people
> —that you are trying to prevent Negro families from
> moving into Deerfield. Reply to these folks that Negroes,
> or any race, creed or color compatible with the tenets
> of the American way are welcome as the flowers in May
> —but this must be on the same terms that are open
> and equal to everyone and are compatible with com-
> munity serenity.
>
> What has occurred, and is occurring, in Deerfield will
> be swallowed up in the sands of time—but if out of it
> all we can help some other unsuspecting community to
> avert such developers, then all has not been lost. Let us
> make so much noise that the world knows what is going
> on here. And in the battle for our individual rights let
> us thank our lucky stars for the unanimity this has forced
> upon us all. Let this town also remember this intrusion
> on its privacy for its history through the ages and to re-
> member forever those individuals who were a party to its
> cause.

Thus spoke Mr. Keller, park commissioner.

Actually, all the "noise" of which Mr. Keller wrote,
which was to let the world know what was going on in
Deerfield, worked in favor of the Residents Association and
the forces opposed to the interracial housing project. Many
people resented all the attention they were getting, especially since much of that attention expressed itself in

critical terms. A sense of martyrdom was engendered, of being the victims of a conspiracy, of fighting the unpopular battle for the rights of the majority.

Help for the anti-Floral Park forces was to come also from the South, after the poll. Some of it was solicited by Lewis, some of it was spontaneous.

For the most part, national organizations and groups had stayed out of the battle, at least in terms of direct action. The National Association for the Advancement of Colored People had not sent in any field workers or literature. This may have been part of a considered strategy, for throughout the entire struggle not a single Negro played an active role.

Some Jews in Deerfield had called the Chicago office of the Anti-Defamation League of B'nai B'rith to ask for advice, and had been advised that there was no need for any particular action as Jews, and that the Anti-Defamation League was "watching the situation." The national church groups took no direct action, except for general statements of policy on integration. Friendship House, a Catholic interracial organization, made available the part-time services of a field worker who was of considerable assistance to the Human Rights group which could not afford to engage its own personnel. The American Friends Service Committee provided literature for distribution, supporting the cause of integrated housing, as did the Illinois Human Relations Council, a state commission, which also gave some staff help.

Except for these few interventions, the "battle of the poll" was fought strictly by Deerfield residents with weapons of their own choosing.

XXIII

It had been announced soon after the November 23 meeting that the poll of Deerfield residents would begin on Wednesday evening, December 2, and close on Friday, December 4. More than 200 volunteers were available, and they were assigned to seven districts. Everybody of voting age was eligible to answer the poll.

When the first announcement was made, the form of the poll had been as follows:

——resist planned interracial subdivision with all proper legal means.
——accept the subdivision.
——abstain from giving an opinion.

In its final form, however, the poll consisted of a small sheet of paper as follows:

UNOFFICIAL AND VOLUNTARY POLL
(Secret Ballot)
1. Do You Favor the Floral Park Subdivision Project? ☐
2. Are You Opposed to it? ☐
Conducted by
North Shore Residents Association
Harold C. Lewis—Chairman.

The dates were also changed, and the actual polling took place on Friday and Saturday, December 4 and 5.

While the preparations for the poll were going on, the newspapers and radio and TV stations were laying down a barrage of stories on their own "opinion polls" based on interviews with private citizens. As the two sides organized, they were to supplement the newspapers' and radio and TV stations' own efforts with official statements, reports on studies, and warnings, to all of which wide publicity was given.

On November 26, the *Chicago Tribune* reported that Mrs. Repsholdt had received two dozen telephone calls to support her husband's stand. That same day, nationally-known columnist Irv Kupcinet, in the *Chicago Sun-Times*, gave public "thanks to persons like Theodor Repsholdt, the Highland Park High teacher who stood up in the face of jeers to applaud the proposed integrated housing development in suburban Deerfield."

"One man with courage constitutes a majority," added Kupcinet.

On November 27, the *Chicago News* carried the first of a series of articles by M. W. Newman, describing the series in this way:

> Suburban Deerfield is in the throes of a crisis over a proposed integrated housing development. The backers of the development have already built two such integrated projects in the East. How do things go in these earlier projects? What has happened to property values? What do the neighbors think? To give the people of Deerfield —and others who may face the same issue—a better understanding of the problem, the *Daily News* has sent one of its top reporters into New Jersey and Pennsylvania to do the story of these integrated projects.

The first story was on a Princeton, N. J., development, and was captioned: INTEGRATED CITY TELLS DEERFIELD: DON'T PANIC. The story went on to tell that few white families had left the interracial subdivision, that the neighbors were happy with each other, that property values had not dropped, but had, in fact, gone up. A second story in the series on the following day said much the same.

On Sunday, November 29, in addition to their newspapers the residents of Deerfield could turn to several radio and TV programs for news and views on interracial housing in their community. At three o'clock a local TV program called *Insight*, conducted by Frank Reynolds, presented a debate between John Hunt and Harold Lewis.

At four-thirty, there was the national Chet Huntley program. At eight o'clock, anyone who had missed the Hunt-Lewis debate could hear it again on radio station WIND, with commentary by a well-known newspaper columnist, Jack Mabley, who was also president of another north shore suburban community, Glenview.

On Monday, November 30, all the newspapers carried stories about the two committees, giving special prominence to the organization of the Human Rights group, and the third of Newman's feature articles appeared in the *News*. The *Chicago American* carried an eight-column spread under the by-line of Peter Reich. It brought to the attention of Deerfield residents the problems of one of its ministers because of his stand on the Floral Park project. The minister was Pastor Berggren of Zion Lutheran Church. "Members of the congregation, including one member of the church board," writes Reich,

> objected to the reporter speaking with anyone at the church, including the clergyman. The board member said he felt the clergyman's stand on the issue was "embarrassing." The clergyman . . . retorted, "If I may put it bluntly, it doesn't make any difference to me who is embarrassed. This is a conviction with me, just as Christianity is a conviction with me. My stand may cost me my job . . . but I was not ordained to serve this congregation but the Augustana Lutheran Church."

The same article carried a lengthy interview with Harold Lewis, repeating and expanding on much of what he had already said publicly and adding the thought that the Floral Park builders and their supporters would do well to be concerned with Negroes "forced to live in substandard housing —instead of those fortunate ones able to afford $30,000 homes."

On December 1 the big item of news was the resignation

from the board of the North Shore Human Relations Committee of Mrs. Willard J. Loarie, one of three Deerfield board members. The organization was already a year and a half old when the troubles in Deerfield began. Progress Development board member Charles Rippey and Unitarian minister Russell R. Bletzer were the other two Deerfield members. Mrs. Loarie objected to the group's endorsement of Modern Community Developers and Progress Development Corporation. All the newspapers carried the story.

XXIV

During the week of November 29, many Deerfield residents received a mimeographed document in the mails, entitled "Membership Application—N.A.A.C.P." The envelopes always bore the return address of some person active in the Derrfield Citizens for Human Rights Committee or otherwise publicly known to be in support of the Floral project. This is the "application":

MEMBERSHIP APPLICATION
N.A.A.C.P.

NAME .... DATE ....
   (use all names you has gone by)
ADDRESS ....
(If living in automobile, give make, model & tag number)
NAME OF MOTHER ....
NAME OF FATHER (if known) ....
NAME OF AUTOMOBILE (Check):
   Lincoln .... Cadillac .... Imperial ....
NUMBER OF CHILDREN
   CLAIMED FOR RELIEF CHECK ....
NUMBER OF LEGITIMATE CHILDREN (if any) ......
NUMBER OF CHILDREN FATHERED (if known) ......
MARITAL STATUS (Check one): Shacked up ....
   Making out .... Worn out .... Still trying ....

GIVE APPROXIMATE ESTIMATE OF INCOME:
From Theft .... From Relief .... From Unemployment .... If you have income from other sources, explain ....
PLACE OF BIRTH (Check one): Charity Hospital ....
Free Public Hospital .... Cotton Field .... Back Alley ....
LIST WHITE SCHOOLS
YOU WOULD LIKE TO ATTEND:
(Use back if more space needed)

....

....

CAN YOU GIVE AS REFERENCE
ANY OF THE FOLLOWING:
Eleanor Roosevelt .... Richard Nixon .... Earl Warren ....
Ed Sullivan .... J. Kasper ....
ABILITIES: Government employee .... Good preacher ....
Agitator .... Slum clearance .... Have razor, Will Travel
(Yes ....) (No ....)
WOULD YOU BE WILLING TO: Serve as Director
of FORD FOUNDATION ...., Director of Urban
League ...., United Nations ...., President ....,
Chairman of Red Cross ....
Are you now or have you ever been associated with any organization that believes in preserving social liberty and democracy by use of force if necessary?

....

PLEDGE
I believe in equality that Niggers is better than white folks is, and that white folks should pay more and more taxes than us Niggers should and us Niggers should have more and more welfare, and now that we has Supreme Court and the U. S. Army on our side, the laws should not be changed no more no how! I promise to praise Eleanor and the Supreme Court and not to snicker when any other disturbed

white folks start crying over how we is persecuted. I
know my rights.

....

The residents who did not get this letter could read
about it in the *Chicago American* of November 30, in
Peter Reich's article, which also spoke of Pastor Berggren's
difficulties. Under a sub-head "Postal Violations," Reich
writes:

> The most rabid segregationists have done their part to
> help matters along by sending out literature such as pur-
> ported "Applications for Membership in N. A. A. C. P."
> These applications ask questions such as . . . [three ex-
> amples are given].
>
> These poison pen letters usually bear the return ad-
> dress of some community leader who has come forward
> in defense of integration. Since affixing another person's
> return address to a piece of mail is a federal offense, postal
> authorities are expected to begin checking on this phase
> of the Deerfield squabble.

XXV

On Wednesday, December 2, leaders of the two opposing groups began to unlimber their big guns. Every
newspaper carried the announcement by Harold Lewis
that the poll would begin that night (this was still on the
basis of the old dates). In the same papers Adrien
Ringuette denounced the poll.

"The purpose of this anti-integration group has now
been brought out into the open," said Ringuette, and
he continued:

> This so-called canvass started out as a fact-finding effort,
> but fact finding is apparently no longer the objective.

Instead the objective is going to be organized resistance. This can have serious consequences. Village authorities could become intimidated into legally depriving a minority of civil rights.

Villagers endorsing the program of these pollsters may discover that they have signed a blank check encouraging unlawful interference with civil rights.

The newspapers also carried the reply by Lewis. "This is simply not the case. The pollsters are going to ask each resident: is he in favor of the project; does he believe it should be resisted or does he prefer not to express an opinion." (This was the first form proposed—it was subsequently simplified.) Lewis then invited the Human Rights group to participate in the poll and to be represented when the votes were counted.

The Human Rights group declined the invitation by announcing a public meeting for Sunday, December 6, the day—as it turned out—that the votes were actually counted.At the same time, the group undertook to study the effect of the housing dispute on the actual sale of houses in Deerfield during this period, and on prices, the results of the study to be announced at the December 6 meeting.

Now a third party made its views known. In Jack Mabley's column in the *Chicago News* that day there appeared this item:

The South watches Deerfield, Ill., with great interest. Here are a couple of sentences from an editorial in the *Atlanta Journal*, which proclaims it covers Dixie like the dew:

"Well, if this (Deerfield) was happening here or some other Southern city, we'd be hearing a lot about ignorance and prejudice and some editor would write a piece about us playing into the hands of Russian propagandists.

"But as long as it's happening where it is, we guess the causes will be explained in terms of economics.

"It is only fair that the whole nation be asked to examine its conscience and stop pointing its finger at the South."

XXVI

On Thursday, December 3, the newspapers reported the announcement by Lewis that the poll would be delayed until the week end because the opinion blanks and the sealed metal collection containers to be used were not yet ready. The same articles announced that the Human Rights group would meet on Sunday.

In the meantime Deerfield residents were already expressing their views in letters to the editors and to reporters. Some people balked at being questioned. Most spoke up freely.

A typical day's reporting in the pre-poll period was offered to Deerfield readers by the *Chicago American* of December 3.

"I guess it's a 'sociological experiment' when it happens somewhere else. When it happens to you, it's downright sneaky."

"But Mommy, you said all people were equal. So why is everybody making all this fuss?"

"I know I have no right to be prejudiced. Yet it's hard to be humanitarian when my life's work is at stake."

The reporter received these comments from a housewife, a little girl, and a realtor in the course of a "pulse-taking tour of homes and businesses." At the end of this tour, the reporter came to these conclusions: "As yet home owners show no signs of panic selling. Talk, yes.

93

But no preparations to do so. The old bugaboo, loss of property values, predominates in the collective fears of white Deerfield. The people absolve themselves of racial bias."

One real estate man told the reporter that people who had signed up for houses in Deerfield were trying to back out. Another agent told him that business was going on as usual.

Residents living along Wilmot Road near the disputed development told the reporter they were not happy about being so close, but none were planning to sell.

The mother of the little girl who couldn't understand the "fuss," since Mommy had said all people were equal, explained to the reporter, "She's too young to understand all the nuances."

The *Deerfield Review* of December 3 devoted its "Deerfield Forum" to excerpts from "scores" of letters they had received. These are the excerpts selected by them:

"If the motivating idea was solely to provide good housing for all the people, could not this development just as easily have been located in a previously non-settled area?"

"We should be as democratic as they suggest and decide this issue in a democratic method—the referendum."

"Why is it so important to have an integrated subdivision in Deerfield? What about the human rights of the people living in Deerfield?" (This one was from Leonard Bronstein, treasurer of the North Shore Residents Association.)

"We are sick at heart to realize that in our peaceful town the rights and wishes of 10,000 people no longer matter." (This was from Mrs. Morris Courington who lives directly opposite the development site and whose husband had announced at the first public meeting that he had been offered half its value for his house.)

"I am convinced that a plan of this nature, forced on

the people by outside groups, will only create friction where none now exists."

"Because I believe this project will make Deerfield a more wholesome community, I would like to express my gratitude to the builders."

"Every house in Deerfield stands to lose $5,000 to $15,000 in valuation or resale value."

"There is considerable national evidence that real estate values are affected less by what the Negroes do than what the white people do."

"I must again urge that these people are in the right, morally and legally."

"Everyone looks upon the Little Rock problem as a national crisis and yet what are the people of our community doing but displaying the same kind of attitudes?"

"We believe the residents of Deerfield will be willing to give of their time and money to fight this thing."

"Deerfield has the unanimous support of all the un-incorporated areas surrounding her in firm opposition to this development."

On Saturday, December 5, the day the poll began, Deerfield readers were reminded that the symbols of their agony, the two model houes on Wilmot Road, had not been worked on since November 13, when Building Commissioner Bowen had issued a stop order. On Friday Bowen had taken reporters on a tour of the buildings, and at least one Saturday paper, the *Chicago American*, carried the comments of the commissioner and Inspector Kilgore, as well as Village Manager Stilphen. The village officials were being neutral on the integration issue. Their pronouncements, as reported by Dorothy Arns to readers of the *American*, said not one word about integration.

From Bowen: "Worst jobs of construction I've ever seen."

From Kilgore: "Even a person who doesn't know a

joist from a stud could tell this is bad construction."

From Stilphen: "The developer has announced publicly that he intends to offer better than average housing for the money. Deerfield hopes to do its part to prove this true. We would like to see every buyer have a perfect house." (The village manager presumably was talking about the building code.)

XXVII

On Saturday, December 5, the poll began.

Lewis had warned the 200 pollsters against "extraneous conversation." They were to hand the resident a ballot, ask him to check whether he favored integration in the subdivision or not, take the name and address of the person polled in order to avoid duplication, and then move on to the next house.

Ringuette had reminded the villagers again that they might be "encouraging unlawful interference with civil rights" by signing for "organized resistance," and continued to work with his committee for a large turnout at the Human Rights group's Sunday meeting.

The sealed containers holding the ballots would be emptied Sunday night at the Jewett Park Field House, and Lewis invited the public to be present for the meeting.

It had been estimated that some 4,500 persons would be eligible to vote. The pollsters turned in 4,045 ballots.

Most of the Chicago papers and a national TV network were represented at the counting. No "opposition" people being present, Residents Association Vice-Chairman Herbert Garbrecht appointed three judges from among non-residents. They were Dorothy Arns, a reporter of the *Chicago American*, and Bernard and Edward Stucka, both of Riverwoods. To open the sealed containers and count the ballots, Garbrecht called for volunteers from among the residents present who had not participated in the canvassing. Eight residents came forward, and the counting began.

It wasn't a particularly tense occasion. The prevailing mood was one of happy confidence. Jim Bade of the *Waukegan News-Sun* described the atmosphere for his newspaper the next day as being "like that of Lake County Republican headquarters as the vote comes in. There was no question about the outcome. The only question was: How big a vote will opponents to the project get."

Of the 4,045 ballots turned in, twenty-two were discarded as "Spoiled." Fifty-six ballots were marked "No Opinion." Of the balance, 3,507 were AGAINST the Floral Park Subdivision Project, 460 were FOR it. 87% AGAINST, 11.4% FOR—eight to one.

Three blocks away, in the Maplewood School at the meeting of the Deerfield Citizens for Human Rights, Adrien Ringuette was telling a quiet crowd of 150 persons that the Human Rights group "was organized to save the good name of Deerfield. It is a cross-section of the community."

XXVIII

Bob Danning knew the results immediately. He had been one of the volunteer canvassers, and he was at the field-house when the ballots were tabulated. He was pleased at the result, somewhat surprised that the majority had been so large. Later, at home, when he told Helen about it, he seemed glad that it was over.

"What happens now?" his wife asked.

"I don't know," replied Bob. "I guess Hall Lewis will

give the Village Board a report, and then it will be up to them."

"But surely he has something in mind, some specific plan, something legal."

"I haven't been in on much of the top-level stuff. From the talk I hear, they will probably go ahead with the park idea—getting the land condemned for park purposes."

"Will you still be busy with the committee?"

"I don't imagine so. There's nothing for me to do. Besides, there won't be any fight now. The poll shows that the village is overwhelmingly on our side. The Human Rights people will probably make a lot of noise, but that's about all they can do. Now I'd say it's between the Village Board or the Park Board and the builders. And that's OK with me!"

Joe and Ethel Robbins heard the results from their jubilant and voluble neighbor Nan Kerwin. Her husband had been at the fieldhouse and had phoned the great news to her before going out with some of the "boys" to celebrate. She had written the exact figures on a scrap of paper which she kept waving at them as she spoke.

"And you know what? They collected almost $6,ooo!" she exclaimed. "That's important, you know. Bill gave them ten dollars. How much did you people give?" She rolled on without waiting for an answer. "It shows that we mean business! Bill says it's all over but the shooting—and we'll do that too if we have to. That's what he said. Isn't he a riot? Well, I guess that will show those Jews they can't shove their Communist ideas down the throats of respectable people!"

And she rushed out to spread the news, completely unaware of the devastation she had left behind her at the Robbins home.

But Not Next Door

The Gilberts had attended the meeting at the Maplewood School. Frank mistrusted the Human Rights group because he had always been suspicious of people who took up causes under such highflown names as "Human Rights," "Equality of Opportunity," "Peace and Democracy." He had never joined the National Conference of Christians and Jews, and he was vaguely suspicious of the United Nations. Besides, he suspected that most of the people in the Human Rights group were Democrats.

Frank and Paula listened in silence, without applauding, as the chairman, Adrien Ringuette, spoke of the need to preserve the good name of Deerfield. Then Dan Walker spoke. He insisted that "a fundamental principle" distinguished this group from the Residents Association, and that was the principle of integration, "despite attempts by the other group to dispute this. . . . They plan to interfere with the right of the builder to build and the people to buy. We plan to stand for those rights."

Dan Walker continued. "I'm not necessarily glad that Progress Development Corporation decided to build integrated housing in Deerfield. . . . I do not welcome controversy." Paula Gilbert nodded her head, and Frank found himself doing the same. "Barriers have been created between friends . . . and the problems of village administration have been exacerbated." Frank agreed, though he was inclined to feel little sympathy for the village officials. "There is an inevitable price of progress, a price I am unhappy but willing to pay. . . . This village has been labelled as insecure, smug, intolerant. I don't think this is true. . . . If we can turn the tide by defeating the park referendum, the world will know that Deerfield has come to its senses. . . . Would we have had a referendum for parks, if Progress Development Corporation had not come here?

Five hundred and fiftt thousand dollars and community
disgrace is the price for these parks."

Frank Gilbert was impressed.

And then he heard his fellow Lutheran Theodor Repsholdt speak of a letter he had received from a prominent
Negro attorney in Chicago saying he would like to live in
the Floral Park project, and Frank felt a twinge of alarm.
And was immediately ashamed.

He heard Sally Burns report that the survey of Deerfield
real estate agencies had showed no effect whatever on real
estate sales in the village.

He heard the chairman promise to investigate the question of whether or not the builders' controlled-occupancy
policy would stand up in court if attacked.

Frank Gilbert had felt like a fish out of water throughout the meeting. He had been with people who were undoubtedly heavily biased in favor of the project, people
who were probably worlds apart from him in their political
thinking (this was his own prejudgment speaking). But
they had been reasonable, they had spoken of law, they
had spoken quietly.

When the Gilberts went home that night, Frank knew
—really for the first time—where he stood on the Floral
Park issue. He had been one of the few who had abstained
from voting in the opinion poll. "They have no right to
do this," he had said to Paula, "to ask for opinions on
a question of law, and do we believe in it or not. They
might just as well poll people to ask if they are for or
against taxes." Nevertheless, he felt now that he should
have registered his opinion—FOR the subdivision.

Frank heard a late radio report that night, giving the
results of the poll. He was not surprised, he was not upset.
When his wife—completely identified with her husband
on this issue as in all others—looked at him with dismay,

he smiled, patted her on the shoulder (a rare gesture for
him), and said: "What did you expect, dear? Now go to
bed."

XXIX

DEERFIELD SAYS 'NO'—SEGREGATION URGED 8–1
POLL OPPOSES INTEGRATION IN DEERFIELD
DEERFIELD POLL NEAR 8 TO 1 AGAINST INTEGRATED PROJECT

These were some of the headlines of Monday, December
7. The newspapers that day also carried a bit of miscel-
laneous information about the Deerfield Citizens for
Human Rights: they had been asked by landlord R.
M. Johnston, a resident of nearby Wilmette, to vacate
their offices by the end of the month. Mr. Johnston denied
that any pressure had been put on him. Nor was he un-
sympathetic toward the Human Rights group, he said. As
an outsider, he simply did not want to get "embroiled in
the controversy."

The North Shore Residents Association leaders were
understandably happy about the results of the poll and
their public statements did not conceal their pleasure. At
the same time, they put the emphasis on the public
service they had performed, a kind of *amicus curiae* role—
to gather information as a basis for the village officials
to act.

Lewis indicated that the results of the poll would be
communicated to the Village Board on an unofficial basis.
This would serve, he said, to show the trustees how the
village feels about the integrated project. Herbert Garbrecht, vice-chairman of the Residents Association, was
more blunt. "This is a clear indication to all of the country
that we are opposed to having an economic stab in the

back," he said. "It is notice to all elected officials and the people of Deerfield that creation of this subdivision would injure property values."

The Human Rights group was obviously unhappy at the results. They certainly were not surprised, except possibly at the size of the majority. But for them the results of the canvassing made no difference whatsoever in the fundamental issue or, for that matter, in what was going to happen in Deerfield. And with the help of the press they made their position clear. ". . . the sampling of opinion taken Sunday by the segregationist group has no bearing on the legality of the issue involved—which is the fact that Deerfield is going to be an integrated community." This was the position of the Human Rights group as expressed by one of its officers, Wesley Wise.

The Reverend Russell R. Bletzer, pastor of the North Shore Unitarian Church and himself a Deerfield resident, had delivered a sermon to his congregation on the poll. The sermon was mimeographed and received wide distribution after the ballots were in. Bletzer was probably the only Deerfield minister who could count on substantial backing from his congregation in his vigorous support of the Floral Park project. His definition of the "real" issues *before* the poll served, for many villagers, as the basis of personal decision *after* the results were known.

The sermon was entitled "Integration Comes to Suburbia." It began by raising the question of the role of religion in modern society. "Can church teachings compete against . . . the cult of success, the striving for status, the need for conspicuous consumption?" "The answer," says Bletzer, "may be about to emerge in Deerfield. . . . The conflict is not really between people of different views It is an inner conflict . . . between conscience and status, between the law of love and the law of the market place, between the dignity of man and the dignity of the dollar. . . .

"Integration in the suburbs is widely accepted as an idea—so long as it happens in some other suburb. . . ."

The minister reviews how the Progress Development Corporation came to Deerfield. "Why was Deerfield selected?" What about the "treachery" imputed to the builders? "The use of the word 'helpless' in some of the publicity of the opponents gives the melodramatic image not unlike that of the ingenue tied to the railroad track, in a 19th century play. . . . A parcel of land, in a village with schools, transportation, water and sewer facilities, was of a good size . . . to build about fifty houses. The price being right, the parcel became the site of Floral Park."

Bletzer goes on to examine the economic factor—property values—in the dispute:

> The emphasis upon economic objections is, I suppose, a sidelong tribute to religious values, and the democratic principles and laws of our country. It is not considered in good taste to object to integration on the ground that one hates all non-whites. . . . Hence, the strategy of opposition is to conceal real motives under socially acceptable masks of reasonable argument: "The builders have come in with stealth; they have imposed their will upon the helpless people of this happy village; they are trying to help Negroes infiltrate this white community; property value will go down. . . ."

Sometimes real hate comes through, says the minister, and he cites examples from the public meetings—the wild accusations: "They"re a bunch of Communists!"; the out-and-out hate of Negroes or white men who would live beside them: "What kind of white people would move into a development like this?" He points out the similarity of language used by Deerfield anti-integrationists and members of the White Citizens Councils in the South.

As to the poll itself: ". . . I suggest that whatever the

results of the poll may be, we are *not* voting on civil rights. That issue has been settled. We are not voting upon the legality of the Constitution. That, too, has been settled. . . . The right of non-white citizens to civil rights is a matter of federal law, and not of village opinion."

On the Village Board of Trustees: "The board has repudiated its commitment to legal rights and procedures, and has abdicated its leadership and authority in village affairs. Leadership has now passed from elected officials to vigilantes. . . ."

Bletzer speaks about the book *Segregation* by Robert Penn Warren—the issue is segregation, the scene is the South. But the problem, the minister says, "is just as common in the North." He offers his congregants two examples from the book, of the roads open to them. The first example:

> "What's coming?" I ask the handsome, aristocratic, big gray-haired man . . . an ornament of the vestry, of boards of directors, of club committees, a man of exquisite simplicity and charm and member of the segregation group.
> "We shall exhaust all the legal possibilities," he says. I ask if he thinks his side will win. The legal fight, that is. "No," he says. "But it is just something you have to do."

And the other example:

> "In a town in south Kentucky, in a "black county" . . . where desegregation is now imminent in the high schools, the superintendent says to me: "The people here are good Christian people, trying to do right. When this thing first came up, the whole board said they'd walk out. But the ministers got to preaching, and the lawyers to talking on it, and they came around." I asked how many were influenced by moral, and how many by legal, considerations.

About half and half, he reckons, then adds: "I'm a Rebel myself, and I don't deny it, but I'm an American and a law-abiding citizen. A man can hate an idea but know it's right, and it takes a lot of thinking and praying to bring yourself around. . . ."

After expressing his hopes that Deerfield will act with reason and maturity, the Reverend Mr. Bletzer closes: "Let us pray: Out of conflict and discord, may we emerge to deeper commitment to brotherhood and love. We would be patient with all who are searching for the way."

XXX

There were many in Deerfield who thought the Floral Park issue was finished, at least as far as their personal involvement was concerned. The village officials knew where the community stood on the issue—it was now up to them. The residents were sure that some legal action would be taken and the Floral Park development would be stopped. And the idea of legal action was comforting to them. The law was impersonal, the individual was not involved. If the law said there should be no integrated housing development in Deerfield, why that was the law's decision, not the individual's.

But their comfort was short-lived. On Monday, December 7, the Deerfield Park Board resumed the session they had adjourned on November 17. At that meeting Joseph Powell, president of the Deerfield Citizens Committee, had "offered to contact local civic groups and to head a committee of such representatives, who would make a comprehensive study of the needs of the entire district, and that in approximately two weeks the study would be completed."

The Park Board had accepted the offer, and the "comprehensive study" by Powell's committee of private citizens was completed. The Park Board was now ready—the day after the results of the poll had been announced—to consider and act upon the findings of the Citizens Committee. The minutes of the Park Board meeting read:

> The adjourned session of the regular meeting of the Board of Commissioners of Deerfield Park District, of November 17, 1959, was re-convened on December 7, 1959 at 7:00 P.M.
> Upon roll call, the following members were present:
>> James C. Mitchell, President
>> Donald W. Keller
>> Aksel Petersen
>> Edward Walchli
>
> * * *
>
> The elections of April and August were discussed. The opinion of the Board was that in each case the land acquisition program had been defeated because it was tied in with other issues that the voters did not favor, i.e. Briargate Golf Course and the swimming pool, and that if presented as a separate issue the program would have carried.
> The Board then proceeded to review the land acquisitions needed for park purposes. The Board was unanimously agreed that the three parcels, i.e. Pottinger Nursery, Adkins Builders and the Jardine Property, which the Board had for some time been trying to acquire, should be acquired. A discussion was further held relating to the need for other property. It was noted that considerable opposition had developed to the swimming pool proposal because of the proposed location in Jewett Park. A decision was reached that two smaller pools, one in the east section and one in the west section, would be more acceptable to the residents. The Board noted that available sites were fast becoming extinct and after reviewing available vacant land determined that the Weinrib's Pear Tree Subdivision with its location on

Wilmot Road (one of the main streets in the Park District) and the old high school site on Waukegan Road (also one of the main streets in the Park District) were ideal sites and decided to include said properties as additional park sites.

The Board then reviewed the Wilmot Park site. It was pointed out that School District Number 110 had been authorized at an election held in August 1959, to build a new junior high school at the Wilmot School Site for sixth, seventh and eighth grades, which would result in reducing available open area at the Wilmot School and Park Site and at the same time increase the school attendance to 1,200 or more pupils on this site with a great increase in sixth, seventh and eighth graders who require large playing fields in their normal athletic, physical and recreational activities. The Board decided that [it was] imperative to acquire additional land. Upon review of the area it was found that the last piece of vacant property of any substantial size located within the Park District and adjacent to Wilmot School and Park Site was the property recently subdivided into the Floral Park subdivision and that said property was absolutely necessary to provide a suitable park area at this location and should be acquired. One member noted that the construction of two houses had been started on the property, but it was noted that only one was very far along and that this building might well serve as a park building. In view of the fact that building was being started on the property it was decided that offers to purchase and condemnation proceedings to acquire both properties . . . should be started immediately so that the value of additional building would not force up the price of the property. It was decided that such action was not necessary on the other parcels as no building was planned on these in the immediate future, but if there should be any indication of such action by the owners, steps should be taken immediately to make offers and start condemnation suits, if necessary.

On Thursday, December 10, the *Deerfield Review*
carried an official notice which read, in part, as follows:

Notice of Election for Deerfield Park District,
Lake County, Illinois

Public notice is hereby given that an election will be
held in and for the Deerfield Park District, Lake County,
Illinois, on Monday, December 21, 1959, at which time
there will be submitted to the electors of said Park District the following question:

Shall bonds of the Deerfield Park District, Lake County,
Illinois, to the amount of $550,000 be issued for the pur-
pose of purchasing or condemning additional land for
parks, building, maintaining, protecting and improving the
present parks and the land to be purchased or condemned
for parks, and paying expenses incident thereto?

The same issue of the *Deerfield Review* listed the six
parcels to be acquired: the old high school property;
Franken Nurseries; the Lowell Builders (Atkins); the
Jardine property; and the Floral Park and Pear Tree subdivisions of the Progress Development Corporation.

Then a statement by Deerfield Park Board President
James Mitchell spelled out the need for parks. The Park
Board, he said, had been very concerned for some time
over the lack of public land for parks. The Deerfield Citizens Commitee had presented long-range plans for land
acquisition, and the Park Board was acting on these plans:
hence, the referendum on December 21. He made the
point that juvenile delinquency "is an almost direct result
of inadequate facilities to take up the idle time of children."

Mitchell's statement closed with the announcement that
"the Park Board members as well as the Deerfield Citizens'
Committee will actively campaign for public support of
this program."

The Park Board had met on December 7, the referen-

dum would be held December 21. The absolute minimum
legal limit for giving notice of a referendum or election
was ten days. But legal notice had to be published and the
Deerfield Review didn't come out until Thursday, December 10.

December 10 to December 21. The agony of personal
decision was not over for Deerfield residents—it still had
eleven days to run.

XXXI

The Park Board said that the decision Deerfield residents
would make on December 21 was about parks. The Human
Rights committee said it was about integration.

"There is other land in Deerfield available for park and
school purposes, and the Park Board had never even considered the Floral Park and Pear Tree subdivisions until it
was announced that interracial housing would be built on
them." This was the position of the builders' attorneys.

"The Park Board was not interested in any particular
piece of property but rather in an over-all program of
land acquisition," was the position of the Park Board.

"Conspiracy!" cried John Hunt.

"Proper community planning," replied James Mitchell.

At the court trial the Park Board president stuck to his
guns. He is on the witness stand being examined by plaintiffs' attorney Kahn.

Q. Are you familiar with the location of the Floral Park
subdivision at the northeast corner of Deerfield and Wilmot Roads in Deerfield?

A. Yes, sir.

Q. Are you familiar with the property cater-corner to
this subdivision, on the southwest corner of the intersection of those streets?

A. Yes, sir . . . Clavey's Nurseries.

Q. Have you ever approached the owner of the Clavey property to determine whether or not all or any part of it was for sale to the Park Board?

Mr. Snyder [attorney for the defense]: If your Honor pleases, I have to interpose an objection here. It is completely immaterial. It is a negative type of evidence.

The Court: I don't see that it is harmful. It is building up the record. Objection overruled. I don't know what it is leading up to. He may have something in mind that he wants to connect up. He may answer the question.

By Mr. Kahn:

Q. Do you remember the question?

A. Would you mind repeating it?

Q. Have you ever approached the owner of this property known as the Clavey Nurseries to determine from the owner whether or not all or any portion of that property was for sale to the Park Board?

A. No, sir, because it is not in the park district.

* * *

Q. Mr. Mitchell, you are familiar with the fact that the Deerfield Park District is authorized by law to purchase property located outside of its boundaries even though it could not obtain that same property by condemnation in the event the seller did not wish to sell it?

Mr. Snyder: Objected to, immaterial.

Mr. Kahn: It is hardly immaterial, counsel.

The Court: I think it is immaterial . . . but he may answer as to whether or not he is familiar with that law.

By Mr. Kahn:

Q. Did you know that—you have been on the Park Board six years, haven't you?

A. That is right.

Q. You have never bought property outside the park district before?

A. No, sir.

Q. Have you ever tried?

A. No, sir.

Q. Were you familiar with the fact that the Park Board could buy property outside of its limits?

A. Yes, sir.

Q. But you never made any attempt to ask the owner of Clavey if he wanted to sell it?

A. No, because we didn't want to buy fifty million bushes or trees or anything else. We felt that the cost of any land of that nature as a nursery would be quite prohibitive.

Q. You mean it is cheaper to buy land with buildings on it?

Mr. Snyder: Objected to.

The Court: We are getting into speculation, what kind of building? A little shack might be of no value, and yet you might have a million-dollar plant. . . . Objection sustained.

Mr. Kahn: I will ask the next question:

Q. Do you think it is cheaper to buy property that has been laid out for a subdivision, improved and has two model homes under construction on it?

A. Than what?

Q. Than to buy a nursery approximately the size of the Clavey property?

A. Yes, sir.

Q. Even though the parcel with the homes would have to be acquired through condemnation rather than negotiation?

A. That is correct, sir.

*　*　*

Q. Have you ever spoken to Harold Lewis at any time about Floral Park?

A. I have talked to Harold Lewis, I have discussed the park district referendum with Harold Lewis, not specifically Floral Park.

Q. When was the first time you discussed the park district referendum with Mr. Lewis?

A. There was a Junior Chamber of Commerce meeting, if you want a date, because I remember that there was a meeting, and I met Mr. Lewis for the first time that evening.

Q. Do you remember when that was, Mr. Mitchell?

A. Only by going back and finding out what the date of that was. I believe it was sometime in December.

Q. This past December?

A. Yes, sir.

Q. Prior to this past December you have never seen Mr. Lewis in person?

A. No, sir, never knew him.

Q. Has Mr. Lewis ever been at a Park Board meeting?

A. No, sir.

Q. What did you say to Mr. Lewis and what did he say to you in that conversation in December at the JC meeting?

A. It was not at the JC meeting.

Q. I am sorry. What was it?

A. It was at a friend's house. I merely mentioned the JC meeting if you wanted a date, because I remember that specifically.

Q. Whose house?

A. Mr. Jursich, John Jursich.

Q. Who was present at this meeting besides yourself and Mr. Lewis?

A. Mr. Jursich, his wife—

*   *   *

Q. What is his wife's first name?

A. That I don't know.

Q. Who invited you to Mr. Jursich's house?

A. He did . . . Mr. Jursich.

Q. Did Mr. Jursich tell you the reason he was inviting you there to meet Mr. Lewis?

A. Yes, sir.

Q. And was it the same day that you went?

A. Yes.

Q. What time did you get the call to go to Mr. Jurisich's, approximately?

A. I would say it was about seven o'clock . . . in the evening.

* * *

Q. And what did Mr. Jursich say to you?

A. He said that there were going to be a number of people over to his house and they wanted to find out what the Park Board was doing, would I be kind enough to come over and discuss the matter.

Q. And what time did you get to Mr. Jursich's home?

A. I would say eight-thirty, quarter to nine.

Q. Who was there when you got there?

A. Just Mr. Jursich . . . and his wife.

Q. And Mr. Lewis arrived shortly after?

A. That is right.

Q. Anybody else show up?

A. A gentleman, a Mr. Mullen and a Mr. Rierson.

Q. Those are two of the defendants in this suit?

A. That is right.

* * *

Q. Tell me what you said to Mr. Lewis and what you heard Mr. Lewis say that night?

A. My reason for going to the meeting, I was curious to see what he looked like, I had never met the gentleman, I was introduced to him, and there was a general discussion of park activities, and I stated that as far as I was concerned, speaking as only one member of the Park Board, that the Park Board had been and always would be for land acquisition for all of Deerfield.

Q. More parks for Deerfield?

A. More parks for all of Deerfield.

Q. Was the Floral Park subdivision particularly mentioned that night by anyone?

A. To my recollection it was not specifically mentioned.

Q. Was the word integration mentioned that night?

A. I doubt that.

Q. How about the word Negro?

A. No, sir.

Q. Didn't Mr. Lewis ask you if the Park Board would consider trying to obtain the Floral Park subdivision pursuant to its power of condemnation?

A. They discussed that particular point, and my answer to that was that the park district was not interested in acquiring any one specific piece of land, that the park district was interested in a land acquisition program for all of Deerfield.

Q. You didn't tell him that the park district was not interested in Floral Park, did you?

A. I didn't say that we were specifically interested in Floral Park.

Q. Did Mr. Mullen or Mr. Rierson say anything that evening?

A. There was a general discussion on quite a number of things. We rehashed and had some conversation about a couple of the previous referendums, particularly the golf course one, which had been a rather interesting situation in the town. In other words, it was a very informal meeting, I would say, and I think that they were curious as to what plans the Park Board might have, and as far as I was concerned there was only one position that the Park Board could take, and that was that the Park Board was not interested in a piecemeal thing, we were interested in a land acquisition program for all of Deerfield.

* * *

Q. How long did that meeting last?

A. Probably an hour, an hour and a half.

* * *

Q. Can't you give us a little better description of what was said by you and what was said by them? It is only five or six weeks ago.

A. Well, there was a lot of general conversation on a lot of matters that I don't think were—I say I don't think, that did not pertain to the area in which you are questioning me on. Of course, for anybody that has not been—

Q. Let us restrict it, then, to the area in which we are concerned in the suit. I am sure that was mentioned.

A. I would say that, as I stated before, there was a question as to what was the park district's attitude or what was the park district going to do, and I again repeat that as far as my conversation was concerned, it was limited to the fact that the park district was not interested in a specific piece of land, that it was interested in land acquisition for all of Deerfield.

Q. That is the best you can remember of that meeting?

A. That is all that I wanted to discuss.

Attorney Kahn could not get Mitchell to admit that the December 21 park district referendum was connected in any way whatsoever with integration, or that the Park Board president had been party to any kind of plot to stop integrated housing in Deerfield by using the Park Board's powers of condemnation. If, as he said, Floral Park and Pear Tree were not discussed by him that evening of December 3 in the home of John Jursich, he had always been interested in these two subdivisions. The ensuing testimony was to establish this interest and what he had done about it:

Q. Can you tell me when the acquisition of Floral Park and Pear Tree subdivisions was first considered by the Park Board?

A. . . . you used the words, Pear Tree and Floral Park. If you want to say when did the Park Board consider that as a piece of land rather than a specific name, we can go back and that was under discussion back in May.

Q. Of 1959?

A. Yes, sir.

Q. Who discussed it?

A. We had a discussion at the Park Board meeting when we had McFadzean & Everly in on their preliminary work for the swimming pool and land acquisition and referendum which was held in August.

The attorney for the builders now addressed himself to the Park Board meeting of May 19, 1959, when Mr. Layman, a representative of the consultant firm of Mc-Fadzean, Everly & Associates, was present. Mitchell insisted that the area now know as Floral Park had been discussed at that meeting. Plaintiff's attorney Kahn was equally insistent that neither of the contested subdivisions had been on the agenda. The minutes of that meeting had been subpoenaed, and he read off the names of the only four properties mentioned in those minutes. None of them referred to the two now designated as Floral Park and Pear Tree.

Mitchell testified that the two properties were again discussed at a meeting of School District No. 110, some time in June, 1959. The meeting was for the purpose of discussing the August land referendum for park-school use and for a swimming pool. The land "around the Episcopalian church," said Mitchell, had been suggested as a possible site for a junior high school, the land now known as Floral Park. It was not included, however, in the August referendum. The Pear Tree subdivision, it seemed, had been considered as a swimming pool site.

Q. What were the results of the August referendum?

A. We lost the swimming pool and we lost the land acquisition.

Q. Where had you proposed to put the swimming pool in the August referendum?

A. As a result of (the) May meeting we had proposed to put the swimming pool in Jewett Park.

Attorney Kahn's next move was to establish the fact that Mitchell had seen the "for sale" signs on the Floral Park property, had been aware that Pear Tree was vacant and available, but had never made any effort to explore the possibilities of buying either one, at least not prior to the announcement of the builders' intention to sell some of their houses to Negroes. How had Mitchell felt when he saw houses going up on this property in which he had claimed such great interest?

A. Well, personally I was very distressed to see the housing going up, because there was a site that the Park Board certainly needed. . . . It means another piece of land was being built up, and there is so darn little land in that part of town that we can get hold of for parks that it appeared that here is another piece of land that is gone.

Q. Until November 17, 1959, did you do anything about your distress?

A. No. We had tried a land referendum in August, and inasmuch as we do all of this work in the evenings or for free, why, we had had two referendums this year, I felt (we) were entitled to a few moments respite from referendums.

Q. You didn't think another referendum this year would be wise?

A. I wouldn't say that. The park district is willing, I would say, to acquire park lands for the good of Deerfield at any time that we can run referendum.

XXXII

Bob Danning didn't have to wait until Thursday to know that there would be a park referendum which would decide the fate of the Floral Park project. He knew about the decisions reached at the Park Board meeting even before the newspapers did. He knew he would have to work on it, to help turn out the vote, to help make sure the referendum carried. He was not overjoyed at the prospect.

The park commissioners had made it clear that the issue was parks. Joe Powell and the Citizens Committee had made it clear that the issue was parks. The village trustees, even the officers of the Residents Association— at least in their public pronouncements—had made it clear that the issue was parks.

Bob Danning tried to picture himself electioneering for additional public facilities which he knew he wouldn't be around to enjoy. He thought of the warning issued by Ringuette and other Human Rights committee spokesmen: "Villagers who sign for organized resistance may be encouraging unlawful interference with civil rights." That was just talk, an attempt to scare the opponents of the project. But for a fleeting moment he wondered if he might be breaking the law in working for the referendum. "Damn it," he thought. "This is the law. The people are going to vote on whether they want parks or not. They've done it before, and now they're doing it again."

Bob hadn't voted in the two 1959 referendums for parks. He knew that both had been defeated. Bob knew he would vote in this referendum. He was pretty sure it wouldn't be defeated.

As he was reading the official announcement of the referendum in the Deerfield Review Thursday evening, his wife asked him if he had heard anything from the New York office about the long-awaited promotion. "Not today," he answered. "But it will come through soon." A few moments later he added, "And the sooner the better!"

Joe Robbins, like most residents in Deerfield, knew about the referendum on Tuesday, when the story was carried in the daily press. "It figures," he told his wife. "Those boys are no fools. They aren't going to mess around with the Constitution of the United States. The people of this town want parks like I want parks! But they figure it's better to have parks and pay a few bucks a year more for taxes than worry about a few dark faces floating around their town. It's smart, real smart."

Ethel was puzzled. "You sound as though you think it's all right to have Negroes in Deerfield. But you voted against the project in the poll, like me, and like everybody else."

"Who said anything about liking or not liking?" Joe was irritated. "So I voted like everybody else. I only said the park deal was smart business."

"Will we vote for the referendum, Joe?"

"How do I know how we'll vote? How do I know we'll even vote? The only thing I know is you can't fight City Hall." And Joe closed the discussion.

As they were lying in bed that evening, trying to fall asleep, Ethel murmured softly, "Joe, let's move." Joe didn't answer.

Frank Gilbert wasn't surprised at the news about the park referendum when he read it in Tuesday's papers. But he was furious when he read the Park Board president's statement in the Deerfield Review on Thursday. He rushed into the kitchen where Paula and Louise were finishing the dinner dishes and read the statement aloud, word for word. "That does it!" he exclaimed. "It's bad enough that they're starting this park issue all over again, but not one of them has the courage to admit that they're out to stop the housing project." (He could never bring himself to say "integrated" or "interracial" housing project.)

"That Unitarian is right," he said. (Paula was shocked. The word "Unitarian" had always been about in the same class as "Communist" or "sex" in the Gilbert home.) "The vigilantes have taken over."

He walked out of the kitchen, angry determination written on every feature. Paula and Louise heard him dial a number on the telephone. "What's come over Dad lately?" Louise asked. "That explosion the other night, now this. And who is he going to tear apart on the telephone now?"

"You mustn't talk about your father like that, dear," replied Mrs. Gilbert in a gently chiding tone. "He's probably calling the pastor."

She was right. Frank Gilbert was telling Pastor Berggren that he wanted to fight the park referendum, and asking his advice on how to go about it.

XXXIII

The news announcing the park referendum didn't create much stir among Deerfield residents when they read about it on Tuesday. Most people had expected something of the sort. And if they still thought that, having expressed their views through the poll, their personal role in the housing dispute was ended, it was because—at the moment—they were too spent emotionally to realize that in less than two weeks they would have to express their views again, and that this time it would be official, with all the consequences of official action.

The principals in the dispute, however, were very stirred and very busy. And a new and unexpected issue arose to complicate matters and to some extent confuse the citizenry. School District No. 109, one of Deerfield's two school districts, had attempted to get two of the properties included in the Park Board's "package" through a referendum of its own on November 14. The School Board (No. 109) had failed by only a few votes, and had scheduled another referendum for January 16. Its president, Paul Greenfield, was not at all happy. "It's a mess," he said. "The Park Board took it upon itself to throw us into this. We want to stay aloof from any referendum not directly connected with our district. They're trying to bring the schools into this problem and it's not a school affair at all." School Board No. 109 could see the gloomy prospect of having the properties it wanted tied up for years in legal entanglements, because these properties were now mixed up with two others in which it had no interest at all, but which were, to say the least, legally and otherwise controversial.

David Whitney, president of School District No. 110, which includes the Wilmot School, announced that he could not "give active support to any master land acquisition program" that did not fit in with the plans or have the approval of Greenfield's district. He made it quite plain, however, that his district would not be at all displeased to receive the two Progress Development properties, one of which happened to be across the street from the Wilmot School. Plans for a junior high school were already on the drawing boards. Whitney, too, foresaw a long legal battle and indicated that he doubted his school district could wait for its outcome to build. "However," he said, "it could eventually be used for playing fields."

At least one person was disturbed by Whitney's willingness to accept the Pear Tree and Floral Park subdivisions for Wilmot School purposes. That was Wells D. Burnette, then a vice-president of Roosevelt University in Chicago, and a resident, like Harold Lewis, of Riverwoods. Burnette addressed a scathing open letter to Whitney, resigning from the advisory committee of School District No. 110 and inviting Whitney to join him in a statement of resignation.

AN OPEN LETTER TO THE PRESIDENT OF THE
WILMOT BOARD OF EDUCATION

Mr. David Whitney
1319 Central
Deerfield, Illinois
Dear Mr. Whitney:

In principle I am sure you will agree with the statement that our schools are the safeguard of democracy. If you did not agree, I am sure that you wouldn't have given the time and attention that you have to Wilmot School in the past few years—especially in trying to keep School District 110 ahead of Deerfield's population explosion.

However, schools in a democracy are more than bricks and mortar. They are more than having enough teachers to maintain a 26 to 1 teacher ratio.

Schools in a democracy must be imbued with the essence of the democratic way of life—a recognition of the dignity and the rights of every human being. Without this over-tone and without the school's paid staff and its lay board providing the right atmosphere by their very own example, our schools will fail. Children soon learn to dis-cern the difference between what we do and what we say.

You and the Board are to be congratulated for your care-ful attendtion to the physical well-being of our children. However, the "unofficial" activities of you and the Board during the past two weeks—and now your official policy as outlined by school superintendent Charles Caruso in a letter to the *Deerfield Review* December 17 (in his capacity as secretary of the Board) gives rise to grave doubts now as to your ability to provide the leadership and example so essential to the training of our children for life in a peaceful, democratic world.

You have told me personally—from the very beginning—of your opposition to the Floral Park integrated sub-division. You have admitted to me your atempts to interest the Board of our second village school district (109) in a move to consolidate both districts with Wilmot providing the entire Junior High School for the village. In this way you felt that a bigger Junior High requiring more land would justify condemning the Floral Park site.

When District 109 would not buy your sceme, you admitted to me that the idea was now being advanced by the almost inactive Deerfield Citizens Committee. When they too failed to involve School 109 in the "integration mess," as the president of District 109's Board described it, you gave your backing to the Park District for the $550,000 referendum and you stated to the press that Wilmot would "not be unhappy" to have the Floral Park site—despite the fact:

——that a very busy state road separates Wilmot from Floral Park

——that the 21 acres will cost $166,000 to condemn although there is much cheaper land contiguous to the school property to the south or across a local road to the west

——that Mr. Trabert [a School Board member] in September assured the P.T.A. that Wilmot had no more immediate land needs—rather that it needed funds to finance a Junior High School building on land already owned by the Board (the Meyer annex area). In fact the architects drawings of the building on this Meyer site were presented

——that a member of the Board presented essentially this same information to its Citizens Advisory Committee in September. To a specific question on need for land there was a specific answer: We are not now concerned with land acquisition. We shall need funds for the Junior High building.

Now add to all this the dual role of Mr. Allyn Franke as both attorney for your School Board and for the Park District.

The situation is pretty bad and I have wrestled with my conscience as to my role as a member of the Citizens Advisory Committee to your Board.

Last year I actively participated in writing the report on problems of teacher retention and recruitment for our school. I was chairman of the committee which prepared the complete report of the Advisory Committee for the School Board. This year I was one of five who volunteered to serve another year on this committee—This time I offered to serve on the sub-committee dealing with improving the public relations of Wilmot school and its Board.

Your official action this week leaves me with little choice. Your involvement of the paid superintendent of our school in having him sign the letter in the *Deerfield Review* is the last straw. When I have lost confidence in both the School Board and the paid superintendent, my only recourse is to resign from the Citizens Advisory Committee and call for the resignation of those who are not only conspiring to defeat integration in Deerfield but are openly using *our school* as a "front" to secure passage of the bond issue. How can I—in good conscience—seek to promote the public relations of the Board and the school administration?

I am also shocked by the audacity of your official statement, "The Board of Education reiterates that it stands ready to provide the same high standards of education for children of all races, creeds, and religions living in the district at the present time or at any future time."

Who do you think you are in stating that you stand ready to "provide" what the laws of the United States and the State of Illinois give you no choice in providing as a public school!

If I could find a single word to describe my feelings at

this time, I guess it would be that I am *ashamed—ashamed* of the people charged with the education of your and *my children*.

Despite all this, I continue ready to serve my school, its teachers, and its educational program and will try in the future (if asked) to serve on committees set up for that purpose. But I cannot continue to serve and advise a School Board in which I have lost confidence.

As an appropriate gesture in seeking to reestablish a desirable moral atmosphere for our school, I invite you to join me in a statement of resignation.

Wells D. Burnette

Apparently School District No. 110's President Whitney did not feel that "a desirable moral atmosphere" was at stake in his negotiations and dealings with the Park Board and the other school district. He did not resign. In fact, Whitney went on to become village president. But Burnette's open letter had added another dimension to the struggle. It had reminded the residents that there were personal decisions to be made, personal decisions that could not be avoided.

XXXIV

One of the favorite stories for after-dinner speakers at race relations conferences is the one about the American, the Englishman, the Frenchman, and the Negro who went into the African jungle to study the life of the elephant. Upon their return to civilization, so the story goes, the American wrote a book about "The Economic Organization of the Elephant Community." The Englishman wrote his book on "The Colonial Policy of the Elephant Kingdom." The Frenchman wrote on "The Love Life of the Elephant." The Negro wrote on "The Elephant and the Negro Problem."

For the villagers of Deerfield, the punch line could easily

have been "The Elephant and Integrated Housing in Deerfield." Few if any Deerfield residents could escape from their "elephant."

A housewife didn't have to be particularly intimate with her neighbor to borrow a cup of sugar, the man of the house needed no long friendship to go next door or across the street to borrow a snow shovel from a neighbor. Not so during the days when Deerfield neighbors were preparing to vote on the park referendum. If you didn't know the neighbor's point of view on Floral Park, you didn't want to risk finding out. If you did know and the viewpoint was opposed to your own, you didn't want an argument. If your neighbor's viewpoint was the same as your own, you didn't want a discussion. There are no statistics to establish the facts, but it could be presumed that there was much less neighborly borrowing going on in Deerfield in December 1959.

Nor was it the cold weather that cut down the number of parties and friendly get-togethers that would be normal to the social life of a suburban community like Deerfield. It was rather the tense social climate. If you invited a few neighbors in for a drink, you couldn't know what might happen. There had already been some pretty violent and unpleasant arguments at such gatherings in Deerfield during this period. And if the people were too polite to argue, the pall of bitter unvoiced feelings hung heavily over the tense group. And if you invited only those who shared your own sentiments, you were consciously excluding some old friends, some of the close neighbors with whom you were in the habit of exchanging invitations. Nor could you escape by inviting only your non-Deerfield friends. Either they gave you gratuitous and usually useless advice, or they made the party sound like a wake with their sympathies and condolences.

PTA meetings, school or church committee meetings,

all the normal organizations and civic activities of the village that were unrelated to interracial housing or any other significant social problem, these too were drawn into the shadow of Deerfield's paramount concern—the houses that might go up at Floral Park. Disagreement about what kind of cookies should be served at the church tea may not have been answered with a tirade on the dissident's racial views, but it was in the minds of the discussants. And if the problem was more important, such as deciding on the speaker for the next meeting of the PTA, one could see the lines being drawn in the committee room, lines that coincided with the members' views on the park referendum. At one meeting of the Deerfield chapter of a national philanthropic organization, a member suggested that the cultural program of the next meeting be devoted to a discussion of integrated housing experiences in the United States. She made it clear that her proposal was intended to help members clarify their own views on the forthcoming referendum. The president replied that in anticipation of just such a request, she had written to the national office of the organization to inquire as to whether or not it was wise to have such controversial programs at this time, and the answer was no. A month before, the chapter had listened to a debate on whether or not Red China should be admitted to the United Nations.

Going to church during these early weeks in December required special effort and determination for many residents. The congregants knew where their pastors stood on the integration issue. Some were not too sure they wanted the pastors to know how they—the congregants—stood on the issue. It was taken for granted that they would have to listen to a sermon dealing directly or indirectly with love of neighbors. And they listened. But they did not go out of their way to stand around and talk to the pastors after the services. Except the few who wanted to congratulate them on their firm support of the principles of brotherhood . . . and the few who wanted to drop broad hints that the pastors should stick to the Bible and leave politicking to the politicians.

Coming home from church was not likely to bring any relief from the pressure of Deerfield's overwhelming preoccupation. If you could suppress momentarily in your mind what your pastor had said or implied about the relationship between Christianity and your vote in the park referendum, the children were there to remind you. If you had avoided any previous discussion of Floral Park or interrace relations in the presence of the children, how did you react to your child's happy babblings about what he had learned in Sunday school in this pre-Christmas season? "Jesus loves everybody, my teacher told me, and I love everybody—like Jews and Chinese and colored people. Does that mean that I have to love Indians too, even the bad ones like on television?" That was easy for one father. He told his little son that the programs on television were just stories and not to be taken literally. He had even forbidden certain programs to the boy because they consistently showed the Indians as "bad." There were just as many bad white men as bad Indians in those days, he had explained. And after all, the Indians had some reason to be angry at the white men because the white men had taken the land away from the Indians.

The teen-agers were more direct—and often more embarrassing to their parents. Many of them did not hesitate to confront their mothers and fathers with their own statements about Floral Park and to ask how they reconciled their words and views with those of the pastor. It was difficult to put off an inquisitive or perhaps troubled teen-age son or daughter with, "You don't understand." And for some parents whose minds were already made up, who knew they were going to vote for the park referendum, there was no pleasure or satisfaction in having their children tell them, "I don't understand the pastor, telling us we have to accept Negroes 'in our midst.' How would he like to have one living next door?"

The parents had great difficulty keeping their views on integrated housing from interfering with their relationships with their neighbors. But the teen-agers—among themselves —managed to disagree and, for the most part, remain friends. Deerfield teen-agers attended school at the Highland Park high schools together with students from neighboring Highland Park and Highwood. The young people probably didn't know or hadn't read in the *Daily News* the Pat-and-Mike story about socialism and the two pigs, but their feelings on interracial housing, as it applied to Deerfield, followed the lines of the story. Most Deerfield students were opposed to the Floral Park project, reflecting by and large the views of their parents. The non-Deerfield students were more inclined to favor the project—in Deerfield, at any rate..

A *Daily News* reporter polled some of the students on the eve of the park referendum. One Deerfield girl said, "My parents don't care but I don't like it." Her girl friend and neighbor said, "I'm for it. My mother is from the South and she has a fit every time it's brought up."

One boy expressed it, "The way I feel about it, all men are created equal. If they want to move out here, all men should have the opportunity." Replied his companion, "I don't think people are going to stand for it. Everybody in my home-room is mad about it. My mom and dad are against it. If a lot of colored people move in, it will turn into a colored section."

A Highland Park girl—a sophomore—said, "It would be a wonderful thing." And a boy—a senior—answered, "So why sweat? I figure they got to come out sooner or later."

The *Daily News* reporter concluded his story on the

interviews by reminding the readers that "If the Progress Development Corporation succeeds in its plan to put up 51 homes and sell 12 to Negroes, the children in the new development will probably attend Deerfield High School, which is expected to be opened next fall."

The parents of Deerfield needed no reminder.

XXXV

The Park Board was now the target of accusations and innuendoes both from within and outside Deerfield, all stating or implying that the park referendum was being used to block integrated housing in Deerfield. Park Commissioner Keller undertook to set the record straight. The referendum, explained Keller, had nothing whatever to do with the proposed integration. The Park Board was simply carrying out the recommendations of a citizens committee, and that citizens committee happened to think that the Floral Park and Pear Tree subdivisions were essential, among other properties, to an over-all plan of parks and school grounds for the community. This was the second time that Keller had had occasion to take the public rostrum to disavow any relationship between the integration question and the plans of Progress Development Corporation. The first time had been on November 27 when he had written his long letter to the *Deerfield Review* attacking the "methods" of the builders.

John Hunt spoke up for the builders. His reaction to the poll had been to advise Harold Lewis to try it again in five years when, he said, "our development will have been occupied for several years and he [Lewis] will have had time to discover what fine neighbors he has and that nothing has happened to depreciate property values." Now Hunt served notice that the builders would fight. The referendum, he said, was "an obvious subterfuge to try to get around the Illinois and United States constitutions. If they proceed with an attempt at condemnation, we will fight it all the way."

Hunt also disclosed another interesting bit of news. The Park Board, with admirable speed and efficiency, had already dispatched to officers of Progress Development Corporation three messengers bearing letters offering $169-999.11 for the two Progress subdivisions and the buildings thereon. The three messengers were Herbert N. Garbrecht, vice-chairman of the North Shore Residents Association; Dr. Leonard Bronstein, treasurer of the Association; and Robert D. Rierson, a member of the board of the Association.

The press, at least, found it interesting and newsworthy that official documents of the village should be delivered by private citizens, specially when those citizens were officers and directors of an organization which had reiterated over and over again that it had no official role or status in the affairs of Deerfield, that its relationship to the village officials was purely "advisory."

The chairman of the North Shore Residents Association, Harold Lewis, did not consider the particular choice of messengers to be of any significance. He explained to a reporter of the *Waukegan News-Sun*: "The letters were to be delivered by the president of the Park Board, but when he had to go out of town he asked these three men to deliver them for him. He picked them because they happen to be his personal friends and they work in the Chicago Loop."

As most people expected, the bids were rejected by Progress Development Corporation. Hunt, in notifying the Park Board of the refusal, warned them, and Deerfield, that another suburban community in the Chicago area, Western Springs, had attempted to acquire land through condemnation when a Negro moved in. The effort had failed.

The Negro was Dr. Arthur G. Falls, a distinguished surgeon who was also the chairman of the board of Progress Development Corporation. Hunt recalled the words of Circuit Court Judge Jacob Berkowitz in handing down his decision: "If this land were condemned, it would become a monument to hate and intolerance. None would care to have such a monument as a playground for children."

Seven years later a Deerfield resident, who had spent most of his life in the recreational field, was to echo the judge's words. After speaking before the Park Board, a few days before the referendum, Bernard Scotch, who lived but a few blocks from the disputed subdivision, said: "If this referendum is passed, it will be the only park in Illinois on which a statue of Abraham Lincoln could not be erected."

XXXVI

While the Park Board and the builders were preparing the battle in the courts, the Human Rights group and the North Shore Residents Association, now with the help of the much older Deerfield Citizens Committee, were preparing the battle for votes.

The major weapon was full-page advertisements in the *Deerfield Review*. Another was leaflets and pamphlets sent through the mails and distributed from door to door. Both sides went all out, with the daily press reporting each move and countermove and expressing itself editorially on the referendum.

The December 10 issue of the Deerfield Review, which carried the official election notice, published a paid advertisement of the Deerfield Citizens for Human Rights. Its message was brief. In large bold-face letters across the top of the page was the challenge: THE ISSUE BEFORE DEERFIELD IS THE LAW OF THE LAND. Then: "Regardless of polls and other side issues, the main issue is clear to all Deerfield citizens who believe in Human Rights. The attention of America is focused on Deerfield. Their question is whether we practice or merely preach democracy." The advertisement then quotes Title 42, Section 1982 of the United States code: "All citizens of the United States shall have the same right, in every state and territory, as is enjoyed by white citizens thereof to inherit, purchase, lease, sell, hold and convey real and personal property."

This was the essence of the December 10 advertisement and it was to be the platform on which the Human Rights group was to campaign for the next eleven days.

On December 17 the Deerfield Citizens Committee fired its biggest gun with two pages of paid advertisement in the *Deerfield Review*. Not one word about integration— not one word about the issue which was wracking the Deerfield citizenry. Or at best, an oblique word, and it was a word that served both sides. The word was "binding," and it was contained in a sentence which was to weigh more and more heavily on the hearts and minds of Deerfield residents:

THIS IS AN OFFICIAL BINDING, LEGAL ELECTION

The rest of two pages was devoted to an explanation of why Deerfield needed more land for parks and a call to vote Yes on December 21 "to save your parks, to improve your village, to increase the value of your homes."

The opponents of the referendum also had two pages in the *Deerfield Review*. One was paid for by the Deerfield Citizens for Human Rights. It began in massive block letters WE JUST CAN'T AFFORD TO BE DEMOCRATIC. This was a quote from a Deerfield resident to a *Time* magazine reporter and which had been printed in that magazine and many newspapers across the country. The message then made several points which were spelled out in considerable detail:

"What does the country think of Deerfield?"

"Isn't the Park Referendum a planned and calculated deception that may cost the citizens of Deerfield hundreds of thousands of dollars?"

"Does this mean we have to keep forever buying land for 'Prejudice Parks'?"

"The Western Springs decision."

"Shouldn't the Park District have invited the public to attend the meeting which proposed the referendum?"

"Isn't the Park Referendum plan a use of 'stealth, subterfuge, and deceit?' "

"In our opinion acquisition of the Floral Park tract is a clear abuse of legislative power."

"Condemnation will not prevent integration."

The page closes with the plea: "Let's not create a monument of hate and prejudice for our children—Vote *No* on the December 21st Park Board Referendum."

The other anti-referendum page was purchased by the North Shore Human Relations Council, which had been founded in May, 1958, and from whose board Mrs. Loarie had indignantly resigned when the organization endorsed the work of Modern Community Developers and its subsidiary Progress Development Corporation. The advertisement called on the Deerfield citizens to vote *No* in the referendum, citing as support editorials in Chicago newspapers, statements of national leaders including the then President Eisenhower, and reiterating that "Our property values will not suffer."

Residents of the troublesome School District No. 109 also bought space in the December 17 issue of the *Deerfield Review*, a modest half-page, but most welcome ammunition for the forces battling the referendum.

SCHOOL DISTRICT 109 DOESN'T WANT IN! the advertisement proclaimed. "The Deerfield Park District in forcing the 'Blank Check' Referendum on us is interfering with the plans of our own School Board to acquire its school sites. We don't want our school plans confused or delayed by the Floral Park legal hassle." There followed a history of the nonparticipation of School District No. 109 in the development of the Citizens Committee's "master plan" for land acquisition, closing with the statement: "The Park Board went ahead with inclusion of school site land for 109, despite objections of our board."

The advertisement is signed "Residents of School District 109," lists twenty-one names, and appeals to Deerfield citizens to "Support your school board—Vote No to the referendum."

XXXVII

On Sunday, December 13, a week after the poll of opinion, a week before the park referendum where the vote would count and would have consequences, the *Chicago Sun-Times* devoted its lead editorial to the growing crisis of decision in Deerfield. Again, the world outside was intruding itself upon the village to tell the residents what others were thinking, what Deerfield residents should think. It was a long editorial. It was resented by most, applauded by some. It defined the issue for all.

DECISION IN DEERFIELD

There are a minority of 460 residents of Deerfield— out-voted eight to one in a weekend poll—who stated their approval of the proposal to install an integrated housing project in their all-white community.

We do not know the exact process of reasoning by which these 460 reached their decision; certainly the circumstances in which it was made did not render it any the easier.

There is the risk—widely alleged, at least—that admitting Negroes to a community diminishes property values.

135

But Not Next Door

There is a widely-held view which this newspaper shares that there was a certain sneakiness in the promoters' failure to disclose their intentions of installing an integrated project until somebody let the cat out of the bag. A great deal less opposition might have resulted if they had been wholly open and forthright. And there would certainly have been less aspect of contrivance if the promoters had chosen a somewhat lower-priced neighborhood, and undertaken to provide housing of a kind more generally needed by Negro tenants—housing below the $30,000 cost bracket. The project at Lake Meadows, openly announced as an integrated development and offering good housing at moderate cost in an area of manifest need, provides such an example.

* * *

But taking the situation as it exists, 460 residents of Deerfield voted against a majority of 3,507 to accept a dozen Negro families as their neighbors, and we presume their thinking ran somewhat like this:

Not only the law, but the spirit of this democracy proclaims equality of opportunity for all citizens regardless of race, color or creed.

We now find ourselves involved, as a nation, in a world situation where race prejudice is simply unaffordable.

It is unaffordable because millions upon millions of people of the brown, black, and yellow races all over the world are asking whether we mean what we profess to mean about respecting human dignity. They are saying that if we can't demonstrate our sincerity at home, we are not likely to mean it abroad, and if that is the case, they'll look elsewhere for their enduring international friendships and associations. These people, these nations, hold the balance of power in the world today.

It is unaffordable, also, because as a nation we are locked into a titanic contest that will require every ounce of talent and energy and dedication we can muster to win. The free spirit that makes that kind of contribution doesn't grow in a ghetto. The Negro, like any other American, will make his best contribution when he can be

136

assured of respect commensurate with his merits—assured of the chance to better himself, to grow, to achieve status in his own right.

*   *   *

We doubt if those among the 460 who followed this kind of reasoning tried to justify their position in terms of dollars; more likely, they simply voted for what they thought was right.

But if an argument is raised on one side that admission of Negroes to a community may prove costly in terms of property values, it is fair to mention the dollar cost of deliberate racial discrimination on the other. It is fair to point out, for example, that the alienation of the friends we need among the non-whites of Asia and Africa can shrivel our markets and cut off our sources of vital raw materials and drastically diminish the prosperity of this nation and all of its people. And it is fair to point out that the ghettos into which we have habitually compressed—and depressed—our minorities have bred crime and ignorance that add hundreds of millions of dollars to the annual tax bill that is shared by every one of us.

*   *   *

What has this to do, specifically, with Deerfield? No more than it has to do with any other community, except that a challenge has been put to Deerfield, to pick up if it will, and in that challenge is an opportunity to take leadership in a constructive solution of a problem that will never cease pressing, in Chicago and other communities, until it is resolved.

One way, espoused recently by Cardinal-designate Albert G. Meyer, is the gradual absorption by white neighborhoods of "a number of Negroes whose social backgrounds, occupations, and standard of living are comparable to that of white inhabitants." This, surely, would be the description of any Negro family able to buy a $30,000 house in Deerfield (and a family unlikely to do any great damage to property values).

The other way is to continue to force all Negroes into ghettos which will then grow and inundate neighbor-

137

hood after neighborhood, compounding the incidence of vice and crime and ignorance and poverty that historically make such areas a financial dead weight on the entire community and a constant threat to law and order.

* * *

We point no finger of scorn or indignation at the majority in Deerfield. The long view is never the easy one to take, and this is one decision that must be made by each individual according to his lights.

But we are glad that there are 460 pioneering spirits in Deerfield ready and willing to move into a new kind of relationship with a group of their fellowmen—ready to give them a chance to prove themselves; ready to assume their basic decency and to accord the respect for dignity they would, in turn, ask for themselves. They may or may not win the day in Deerfield, but they are providing moral leadership that will, here and there, cause others to re-examine their own consciences and their own reasoning. The impact of their kind of leadership will grow—is growing—in the South as well as in the North. Some unmeasurable but substantial share of the hope for a secure America in a peaceful world depends upon how swiftly their viewpoint spreads among their neighbors all over the country.

XXXVIII

As election day approached, both sides stepped up the attack. The Human Rights group and its supporters were fed ammunition by a score of sympathetic organizations in the Chicago area, and they could draw on the editorial pages of the Chicago dailies and newspapers all over the country for more.

The North Shore Human Relations Committee mailed out a three-sheet summary reviewing all aspects of the Deerfield situation.

The American Friends Service Committee prepared a

two-page montage of news clippings from the Chicago dailies and other newspapers, with heavy emphasis on editorial comment.

The Catholic Interracial Council had already supplied a field worker who had rendered invaluable service to the pro-integrationist forces. The Council had also conducted an investigation of the unofficial opinion poll, and their highly critical findings of both the method and objectives of the poll were now brought into play to attack the anti-integrationists.

The Chicago Presbytery called upon its 300 ministers and elders of 143 churches in the Chicago area to support "a non-segregated church in a non-segregated society," and publicly urged the Presbyterian Church of Deerfield and its interim minister to "continue a ministry of reconciliation in the midst of community controversy, deploring any emphasis toward hysteria, fear, repression or economic boycott."

The Church Federation of Greater Chicago gave strong public backing to the Floral Park project, pleading with Deerfield not to "segregate itself from the march of historical processes which are now moving with seeming irresistible force toward justice for all and especially for those who in the past have consistently been discriminated against."

The Deerfield Citizens for Human Rights had some ammunition of its own, to supplement the very welcome support from outside the community. They prepared and gave wide distribution to a "Questions and Answers" leaflet which reminded the villagers of three land acquisition proposals they had rejected at the polls since April, 1959, and which closed with a strongly-worded legal opinion by Donald S. Frey, chairman of the zoning committee of the Illinois State Bar Association, and an expert on municipal law. "Any action by the Park District of Deerfield to bring condemnation proceedings against the property already owned by the Progress Development Corporation, planned for an integrated housing development, would constitute an unlawful abuse of the Park District's power of eminent domain."

This legal opinion was further supported in a statement published in the *Deerfield Review* and given wide publicity and distribution by the Human Rights group. The statement was signed by sixteen practicing members of the Illinois bar, all residents of Deerfield. It urged citizens to vote *No* on the referendum.

The Human Rights group kept up the barrage of printed words right up to the last moment, quoting editorials, citing studies to show that Deerfield home prices had held up during the current crisis, and above all stressing that integration was coming to Deerfield, if not now, later. But coming it was, they said, because it was consistent with the law of the land and with human dignity, and nothing could stop it.

The North Shore Residents Association distributed only one printed piece of literature, a large single sheet crowded with copy as though the authors wanted to be sure that they said everything this one time and that nothing was left out. It was entitled FACTS YOU SHOULD KNOW ABOUT THE DEERFIELD PARK BOND ISSUE REFERENDUM TO BE HELD MONDAY, DEC. 21, 1959. The leaflet begins by disavowing any concern with the referendum.

> It has come to the attention of the North Shore Residents Association that much misinformation has been circulated concerning the referendum and other aspects of the problem with which the community is now faced. Although the subject of the referendum is not the concern of the Association, its officers feel a responsibility to Deerfield citizens to share its information, in order that all

decisions reached will be based upon the truth. The following questions and answers may be of help . . .

It then lists five questions, and again, in reply to the second question, the Residents Association detaches itself from the issue of the referendum. Answering its own question about the need for parks in Deerfield, the leaflet states: "Although it is distinctly beyond the province of this Association to express any opinion on this subject . . ." and then goes on to give the appropriate section of the study done by the "Fact-Finding Committee of the Deerfield Citizens Committee."

Throughout the document not one word is said about integrated housing or racial issues. One of the sections deals with the question of property values in the areas near "the housing projects located in the East that were put up by the builders now seeking to locate in Deerfield." But not one word to indicate that these projects were interracial.

Nor does the leaflet tell the villagers which way to vote. The Association is neutral to the bitter end. It simply calls on the citizens of Deerfield to "*Beware* of rumors . . . that may be circulated at the last possible moment to influence your vote on the referendum. If in doubt, call any officer of the Deerfield Citizens Committee, Village Officials, or officers of this Association. . . ."

Certainly the most dramatic piece of writing in the battle of the printed word was done by Harold Lewis himself. It was distributed on the eve of the referendum, on the week end of December 19 and 20. It consisted of a single large sheet, eleven by sixteen inches, with practically every square inch covered by copy in very small type. Its very form carried impact, as did its title, THE MASSIVE WALLOP!

Lewis makes it clear at the very beginning that he is writing as an individual. "For a moment I would like to step aside as Chairman of the North Shore Residents Association," he says,

> to make several personal observations that bear on the problem now facing this community.
>
> Although we have made it clear that integration is *not* the issue, our opponents continue to insist that it is. A carefully contrived pressure campaign has been directed at Deerfield citizens. . . . I can find no other case where outside forces have been marshalled, on such a gigantic scale, to interfere in a purely community matter and to confuse and intimidate its citizens. The pages of history must surely record this cowardly attack on a tiny village with shame and scorn. Conversely, the way that Deerfield citizens have remained steadfast in the face of this 'massive wallop' will be long remembered. That kind of courage is the stuff of which *real* Americans are made.

The tract then deals with "The Religious Aspect." "*It is a fact*," he writes, "that within each denomination there is considerable disagreement concerning our religious duty in connection with the subject of integration vs. segregation." To support this point, Lewis cites at some length a "scholarly" address entitled, "A Christian View on Segregation," by "the most highly regarded" Dr. G. T. Gillespie, D.D., President Emeritus of Bellhaven College. Dr. Gillespie says, quotes Lewis, "The principle of segregation may be defended on Biblical grounds, and is not un-Christian."

Under the caption "Continued Deceit," Lewis discusses briefly what he terms the "*real* issues in this controversy." He devotes most of his attention to the advertisement in the *Deerfield Review* entitled "School District 109 Doesn't Want In" and signed "Residents of School District 109." This "ad" Lewis terms a "callous and calculated effort to again deceive the community" by conveying the impression that the twenty-one signatories were expressing the official views of School Board No. 109.

The next section is entitled "The Supreme Court" and begins:

> Of much deeper import than integration or our local problem is the extent to which Communist and extreme left-wing elements are penetrating all phases of our daily life. . . . Unfortunately, of recent years, left-wing philosophies have influenced certain political appointees to our highest tribunal to the extent that Constitutional Law has been discarded in favor of personal opinion and psychological theories that may be disproved tomorrow.

Chief Justice Earl Warren is the main target here, for his opinion handed down in the Brown case, which Lewis does not explain, assuming—presumably—that his readers are informed about the case.

The closing section is entitled "Usurpation of Power." "What was once legal is now illegal by judicial usurpation of legislative power. In effect, the Constitution has been amended without consent of the States or the people." There is a quote from George Washington's Farewell Address, and then Lewis relates everything he has written to Deerfield in these closing remarks:

> Perhaps we in Deerfield have a date with destiny. Perhaps reserved for us is the honor to strike a blow in defense of government "of the people, by the people and for the people." We must not allow ourselves to confuse the issue of integration with the proper exercise of a municipal right. The project that has been the source of controversy is but a manifestation of the usurpation of power already worked upon the nation. As such it must not be permitted to become the symbol of *any* cause, no matter how loudly it may proclaim itself. Above all,

the rights of the people must be protected.

It is my earnest hope that the foregoing will help all of us to see the real problem in its proper light and will afford further justification for our stand—though none is really needed. Finally, I am happy to report that letters have poured in from all over the nation offering encouragement and support. It is heartening to have tangible evidence that we are not fighting alone and that the great common sense of the American people has pierced the veil of deceit.

THE MASSIVE WALLOP! was withdrawn after reaching about a fourth of the families in Deerfield.

XXXIX

The attorneys for the builders must have considered "The Massive Wallop" an important element in their case against Lewis, because they introduced it as evidence in the court trial. Along with it, they introduced another interesting bit of evidence, a letter dated December 16, 1959. It was signed by Harold Lewis, and was a grateful acknowledgement of help received. This is the letter as reproduced in the court record:

Association of Citizens Councils
Greenwood, Mississippi
Gentlemen:

I want to express my deep appreciation for the material sent to me last week, pertaining to the problem of integration. I have studied it carefully and am convinced that your approach to the problem will command respect. The absence of prejudice or emotionalism lends great credence to your arguments.

You may be interested to know that a week ago the North Shore Residents Association polled Deerfield residents to determine how many favored the integrated project and how many were opposed. The tabulation of ballots showed that 460 favored the project with 3,507 opposing; 56 expressing no opinion. It is my feeling that this ratio would prove to be typical of residents anywhere in the North if confronted with a similar situation. The impression that you may have that the North is trying to force integration down the throats of the South is understandable, although false.

It is my personal opinion that there is little sincerity on the part of either Northern politicians or news media in their advocacy of integration. It is purely political. I gather that both parties are anticipating a fairly evenly divided white vote in the next national election, which, if confirmed, would put the balance of power into the hands of the negro voters. The result? Each party is trying to outbid the other to attract votes. A recent article in the *Chicago Daily News* pointed out that Democrats are concerned about the defection from their ranks by negro voters during the last two national elections. It further stated that even a stronger civil rights platform is under consideration.

It has been most difficult, almost impossible, to get an even break from news media in reporting of our Deerfield problem. As you have probably observed, crushing pressure is being brought to bear on us by church groups and many other organizations seeking to impose instant and compulsory integration. In spite of all this, the Deerfield citizenry has thus far remained united and determined to resist at any cost. I only hope that nothing will happen to change its mind.

I would imagine that determined resistance would be easier to maintain in the South than in the North, although the consequences of defeat would be far more devastating. At least you do not have to fight your political leaders and ministers and newspapers to the extent that we must up here. Any support that you can give us will be most helpful. A little encouragement now and then can be strong medicine for an embattled village. The technique being employed by Modern Community Developers, Inc., of Princeton, New Jersey, and its wholly owned subsidiary Progress Development Corporation is based upon a stealthy approach to a community, a conspiracy to deceive its government and residents until it is too late and then the marshalling of great pressure to force compliance. We in Deerfield feel an obligation to other helpless communities to defeat this project lest it becomes an approved technique for the destruction of other communities. We shall do our best.

In the meantime, if it is possible to raise a few prominent voices in our behalf, we shall be forever indebted to you.

Sincerely,
H. C. Lewis, Chairman,
North Shore Residents Association

Whether or not the residents of Deerfield felt themselves to be a "helpless" community, the image of an embattled citizenry in desperate need of assistance could not have evoked much sympathy from at least one Mississippi citizen, a Congressman, who several weeks later turned to Deerfield for help. The *Deerfield Review* of February 25, 1960, carried on its front page a story describing an interesting (very few Deerfield residents could find it amusing) sequel to the Lewis letter.

The story is headed: "Mississippi Congressman Asks Deerfield To Find Housing For 150 Negro Families." It goes on:

> Joseph W. Koss, Deerfield Village president, has received a telegram from Washington, D. C., prepaid at government expense from John Bell Williams of Raymond, Miss., a member of Congress, 4th Congressional District of Mississippi, in which he asks if Deerfield can accommodate 150 Negro families.

146

The telegram is dated Feb. 18, 1960, and is as follows:

Passage of the new Civil Rights bill now appears certain. There is no question but that the passage of this legislation will aggravate racial friction previously fomented by the Civil Rights Act of 1957 and a series of Supreme Court decisions.

This means, of course, that the exodus of Negroes away from Southern States into already integrated northern cities will be accelerated to a considerable degree. While we in the South do not question the Negroes' right to migrate to other sections of the nation, we are very much concerned over their future welfare.

Your help is urgently needed in setting up a citizens' committee for the purpose of assisting these Negro citizens in their re-location problems, particularly with respect to finding suitable employment, adequate housing facilities, etc.

Please advise, by wire collect, whether you would be willing to cooperate toward the end that 150 additional Negro families might be comfortably accommodated in your city of Deerfield.

The same newspaper carried the half-page paid advertisement of six clergymen and the Deerfield Citizens for Human Rights inviting the villagers to attend a meeting for Deerfield's Brotherhood Week observance. "Brotherhood, Neighborhood and The Law" was the announced theme of the meeting.

The newspaper did not indicate how Village President Koss had replied to Mississippi Congressman Williams.

XL

Newspapers and magazines, radio and television kept the nation and the world informed about what was going on in Deerfield. The people of Deerfield knew it, and didn't

like it, not one bit. They had been told—by both sides—
that their decision on December 21 would affect the
nation, perhaps their country's place among the nations
of the world. It was a responsibility they didn't want.

Newspaper reporters questioned them, interviewed their
children, microphones captured their words, television cameras their faces—and their words spoke back to them and
their faces stared back at them from their daily papers
and their television sets.

When they went to work in Chicago, they were questioned again, and they were quoted to themselves, and
they listened to jokes about themselves.

The residents of Deerfield were tense and unhappy as
the day of decisions approached.

A number of isolated incidents in the few days before
the voting added to the tension and at the same time
reflected it. The School District No. 109 affair with its
Greenfield-Whitney-Park Board imbroglio added fuel to
what was probably an old fire. The Burnette attack and
resignation fanned the flames and added a personal element to the general controversy.

What may well have been simple misunderstanding
helped intensify the bitterness between the two sides.
Charles Rippey, as a director of Progress Development
Corporation and a resident of Deerfield, asked to see the
Park Board records and minutes, in order to determine
whether or not the disputed sites had ever been under
consideration by the Park Board. It took him three days
to get them. Chicago newspapers implied that Catherine
Price, Village and Park Board secretary, was preventing
Rippey from seeing the records. When she did make them
available, she insisted that the Park Board attorney be
present, evoking further resentment by the developers and
their supporters, since the records were public property.

A *Chicago Daily News* columnist, Tony Weitzel, in an

article too aptly titled "More Fuel for Deerfield Tinder-box," wrote that somebody had "smuggled in copies of a Negro paper."

"It carried a story," the Weitzel tidbit continues, "that Deerfield already has one colored couple (passing as white) and that a poll-taker visited them, asked them to vote on the burning issue, and remarked, 'How would you like your sister to marry," etc. . . ."

Name-calling became more common. Jack Lemmon, in a debate with Harold Lewis before 100 members of a north suburban home owners association, described the opponents of the interracial project as "neo-fascist vigilante segregationists." (The Reverend Mr. Bletzer's designation of the North Shore Residents Association as "vigilantes" was catching on.) In the same debate Lewis was quoted as saying in response to a question from the floor, "I wouldn't be telling . . . the truth if I didn't admit that having Negroes is one of the basic issues." Also, that he didn't care what the rest of the world thought about Deerfield opposing integration. "I am tired of the United States having to explain everything it does."

By the time the supporters and opponents of Lewis were through saying "He didn't say it," "He did say it," they were yelling "You did say it," "I didn't say it!" And the word "liar" was getting heavy circulation, some of it across once friendly backyard fences.

The two model homes were a constant source of tension, a constant reminder of the basic issue. They became, in their own right, a subject of further dispute. Four days before the election, a carpenter discovered that in one house seventeen studs supporting the roof had been chopped through, and two in the other model house. The builders were excited, and wanted investigations, also protection for their property. Police Chief David Petersen apparently saw no reason for concern. "I don't know why they're getting so shook up about this," he was reported as saying in the *Sun-Times* the next day. "We've had vandalism at housing projects here before, and usually it's just kids doing it." He went on to suggest that the builders were "looking for publicity."

The villagers never knew—nor apparently did the builders—whether the model houses would ever be finished or not. For three weeks after November 13, all work had stopped. Then work was resumed. Another infraction of the building code stopped it again. Vandals came along and permission was granted for necessary repairs. Then there was confusion about a technicality called "spot surveys" and the red stop orders were posted again. Obviously, the completion of the two buildings would not affect the outcome of the basic struggle one way or the other. But every nail that was driven brought joy to some and misery to others. The very starkness and skeletal appearance of the houses added a somber note to the general atmosphere.

Just how much taxes would go up if the referendum were passed added another element of worry to already worried residents. A Park Board official had estimated that park district taxes would go up by seventy-five percent in a few years. In point of fact, this would mean an increase from about $21 to $34 per year for most homes. Those who opposed the integrated projects and who knew their arithmetic and taxes reckoned that $13 per year was not too much to pay to keep integration from their doors. But for less sophisticated residents, taxes were taxes and a seventy-five percent increase was a whopping big increase.

The children were not immune from what was happening to their parents, although in most instances what they did in the situation was what their parents told them to do, and what they said was what they heard their parents say. Certain children discovered they weren't allowed to play with youngsters who had been their constant playmates for months and years. One child, the son of an active member of the Human Rights group, was told by a former companion, "I can't play with you any more, because your father cost my father ten thousand dollars." Another child calmly announced to her playmates, "Abraham Lincoln was a Jew—my mother told me."

There had to be at least one touch of melodrama in the situation, and it was provided the week end before the vote. The villagers involved, however, did not look upon the affair as melodrama. On Friday morning, some children on their way to the Wilmot School found a large wooden cross on the lawn of the home of Bernard Scotch, who just three days before had sharply attacked the referendum before the Park Board. The cross, about four by six feet, was charred as though it had been set on fire, and resembled, according to the police, the type used by the Ku Klux Klan in the South. Mrs. Scotch is an active member of the steering committee of the Human Rights group, and she made no bones about how scared she was by the incident. She also made it clear that she would continue working to defeat the referendum. Very few of the immediate neighbors came over to the Scotch home to express their concern. One person—a stranger to them—telephoned, after reading the story in Saturday's newspapers. He lived on the other side of Deerfield, and he called to express his indignation. "I don't go along with you on this integration business," he said, "but I sure as hell don't go along with this KKK stuff!"

XLI

On Monday, December 21, 1959, the citizens of Deerfield turned out to vote. They turned out in the greatest numbers in Deerfield history. There were no names to choose, no multiplicity of items to mark. The ballot was

small for there was only one question before the voters,
only one box to mark:

Shall bonds of the Deerfield Park District, Lake
County, Illinois, to the amount of $550,000 be is-
sued for the purpose of purchasing or condemning
additional land for parks, building, maintaining, protecting and improving the present parks and the lands
to be purchased or condemned for parks, and paying
expenses incident thereto?
YES ☐   NO ☐

The lines in front of the polling places were long, and
people waited silently and patiently for their turn to vote.
They knew what they were voting about. It wasn't parks.

They had known what they were voting about just two
weeks before when they had marked other ballots asking
whether they were for or against the Floral Park subdivision. But then it hadn't really mattered. Or it had mattered
to the extent that it might have helped bring about this
referendum. And they knew that the referendum might
have come about anyway. They knew that this vote mattered, that this vote would have consequences. This vote,
as someone had said, was "binding."

For weeks now, no Deerfield resident had known what
it meant to be alone, really alone. His neighbors and the
nation had been with him constantly—in his living room,
on his train, at his job. Now, in a tiny curtain-bound
cubicle, each resident was alone, alone to make a simple
cross in one—and only one—of two little printed black
boxes.

Now each Deerfield resident was stripped of rationaliza-
tions, of pressures, of support.

Alone with the truth.

But Not Next Door

Bob Danning and his wife voted separately, he in the morning before going to work, she at lunch-time because the children were eating with neighbors. Bob knew how he was going to vote, and this time he knew why. He marked his ballot without hesitation, confident for the first time that what he was doing was right. He was not a man of prejudice, and he emphasized the not as he reasoned it out. He was not a bigot. He believed in "live and let live," and that was just the point: the developers of the Floral Park subdivision did not believe in "live and let live," and his vote for parks today, parks he would never use, was a vote for the right of the majority not to be imposed upon by the minority.

Helen Danning had not slept well the night before, and she had been envious of Bob being able to sleep so soundly there beside her. Bob was so sure. She was not. She had a twenty-minute wait before she entered the voting booth, and she stood there motionless for what seemed to her an eternity. Finally, she placed the ballot, which she had been holding in her hand all this time, on the ledge-like table, and marked her cross in the box marked Yes. She was as confused and disturbed when she came out of the booth as she had been when she went in. But it was done. Where her own judgment and values were not equal to the decision, she had to rely on Bob's. Now she could go home and pray that Bob's promotion would come through quickly.

Joe Robbins had intended to vote before going to work, and he had left the house a half-hour earlier in order to vote and still be in time to open the store. He started to drive towards the polling place in his district, changed his mind, and drove on towards Eden's Highway and his place of business. He still hadn't made up his mind. His friend

Fred came in during the morning, and Joe tensed himself for the onslaught. It didn't come.

"You came early this morning," Fred said. "I was early myself, and I saw you. That means you didn't vote yet. It's tough, Joe, it's tough. You want to vote for the underdog because you think that's the right thing, the moral thing, and besides you're a kind of underdog yourself. At the same time you don't want to hurt your neighbors, maybe even your friends, because they're nice people and why should you do something that makes them unhappy even if that something doesn't bother you especially. And you can't not vote, because you're a responsible man. It's tough, Joe."

Joe was dumbfounded. Such sympathy, such understanding from Fred Bernstein? He had underestimated his friend's capacity for kindness. After Fred left, something he had said stuck in his mind. ". . . because they're nice people." Were they all such nice people? Was Nan Kerwin so nice? Not because she had talked about Jews—it had been obvious that she didn't know what she was saying, not that stupidity was an excuse. But she was the biggest gossip in the neighborhood. She and her husband had talked—not talked, shouted—through this whole business like leaders of a lynch mob. These were nice people? And that "Massive Wallop" thing: that was nice?

Joe quickly phoned his wife. "Ethel," he shouted into the mouthpiece. "Go quick and vote. And vote No, do you hear?" "But I voted already, Joe, and I voted NO, but I didn't need you to tell me. They want parks, they can buy them without my money. And if you listen to me, we won't ever need their parks!"

Joe laughed, and his laughter was almost hysterical. "All right, all right," he told his wife. "I'll see you at home and I'll listen to you. But I'll be a little late. I have to vote."

Frank Gilbert didn't go to his office on Monday. He had been busy all week end making telephone calls to bring out the voters, trying to persuade them to vote against the referendum. It had been an exhausting experience because he had never done this sort of thing and he had been as uncomfortable on the twentieth call as he had been on the first. He had voted early, and remained at the polling place to take assignments from his district Human Rights chairman to pick up people in his car and bring them to the polling place, in case transportation was needed. He was there when his wife arrived to cast her ballot. He had not spoken to her about her vote. He assumed she would vote against the referendum because he was against it, but he wished that this time she would make up her own mind.

Paula smiled at him as she stood in line, waiting her turn. "Don't worry, dear. Your side is going to get another vote," she said. Frank almost muttered his answer, because there were rules about electioneering at voting places, and he saw no reason to consider this situation an exception. "You mustn't vote against it because of me," he said. "This is the kind of decision you must make for yourself." And he was self-conscious as he said it because it sounded so pious, and he didn't really mean it. Paula answered him. "If you're for it, I mean against it, and the pastor is against it, and if you don't mind having Negro neighbors, then that's good enough for me." And she moved on with the line.

As she entered the voting booth, she smiled again. As though she could possibly think anything contrary to Frank's views! Frank was always right.

XLII

Out of 4,066 voters in Deerfield, 3,865 cast ballots. The

vote was 2,635 FOR the bond issue, 1,207 AGAINST. Just over two to one.

XLIII

Deerfield had voted, and the whole nation had waited eagerly for the result. Deerfield had waited too, but not eagerly. Many villagers sensed that their community would never be the same again, regardless of the results. The same newspapers that reported the returns on the election carried other stories and announcements that proved them right.

One expected announcement came from John Hunt. "I am disappointed only because it means an expensive court fight," he said, and served notice that the builders would fight to the finish. Park Board President Mitchell announced the name of the firm that would handle the condemnation proceedings.

Edgar Crilly, a former member of the vestry of St. Gregory Episcopal Church and a new recruit to the Human Rights group steering committee, released a letter from the White House signed by Presidential Assistant E. Frederic Morrow. Crilly had wired President Eisenhower no November 29 (before joining the Human Rights group), and expressed concern over the opposition to the integration project in Deerfield. The wire asked for "professional assistance." Morrow's reply read, "It is encouraging to the President that you and others have concerned yourself with and are asserting leadership toward protecting a basic American principle of fair dealing, in whatever respect, with all our citizens." The letter went on to say that the President had asked Federal Housing Administrator Norman P. Mason to study immediately the situation in Deerfield.

Pastor Berggren said, "If we in Deerfield could send an

apology to freedom loving people all over the world, we should do so." James Mitchell said, "The vote means every Deerfield resident will have a park or park school site within a mile and one-half of his home."

Adrien Ringuette announced, "We are saddened at the defeat of morality, justice, and reason by the organized power of prejudice. Deerfield voters have committed themselves to a long, expensive and, we believe, futile legal fight." Joseph Powell said, ". . . it was unfortunate that the bond issue had become involved with the racial question. Ten years from now the voters will be glad they approved the bond issue."

The newspapers of the North said, "Shame!"

The newspapers of the South said, "Now look who's talking!"

The residents of Deerfield said they had had enough of citizens committees for and against, of controlled-or uncontrolled-occupancy building developments, of newspapers, radio, television, leaflets, hand-outs, elections, and of responsibility for the national morality and their own.

And of parks, too.

XLIV

The Deerfield story is still unfinished, but most of it is now being told in the courts, and it will be some time, possibly years, before the concluding chapter of that phase is written.

The Park Board had little trouble getting its condemnation proceedings completed in the Lake County courts. The builders' appeal was rejected.

But prior to this, the builders lost no time in filing suit in federal court against those they considered involved in the "conspiracy" against them. They sued on three counts involving twenty-one persons: all the members of the Village Board of Trustees, all the members of the Park Board, Joseph Powell and Andrew Bradt of the Deerfield Citizens Committee, and Harold Lewis, Herbert Garbrecht and all the other officers and directors of the North Shore Residents Association.

The three counts consisted essentially of the request for temporary injunctions against the park and village boards to stop the condemnation process and any interference with the construction, and a claim against all the defendants for $750,000 in damages.

A lengthy preliminary hearing was held in the United States District Court for the Northern Illinois District, before Judge J. Sa mPerry. On March 4, 1960, he handed down his decision—in favor of the dependants on all three counts.

Judge Perry could find no evidence of "conspiracy," nor that the civil rights of the plaintiffs had been "impaired or jeopardized." The "controlled-occupancy pattern," he ruled, was illegal, "and the plaintiffs do not come into a court of equity with clean hands." He interpreted the Park Board referendum to be simply an astute political stratagem which took advantage of prevailing hostility towards the Progress Development projects to get a bond issue passed for land for which he considered genuine need had been established.

His memorandum of decision concludes: "The decision upon the facts in this case can be of no comfort to any group of individuals or to any community which might violate the civil rights of Negroes or other minority group members. This case is decided upon the facts as established by competent evidence in this particular case—facts that completely overcome the unsupported allegations of the Complainant therein."

The builders promptly appealed the decision.

On January 4, 1961, the United States Court of Appeal

ruled that the builders were denied the right to prove that their civil rights had been violated by the halting of their building projects. The court remanded the case to Judge Perry and ordered that the builders be heard on their charge that they had sustained $750,000 damage. The Appeals Court ruled further that Progress Development Corporation had been denied the right of trial by jury. The ruling was unanimous on the part of all three judges.

In any event, it was all to do over again before Judge Perry, this time with a jury. (Judge Perry subsequently asked that the case be assigned to another judge so that there might be no question of prejudice.)

The officers of Modern Community Developers and of Progress Development Corporation were delighted with the Appeals Court decision. The initial reaction of the village officials was "No comment," as they went into a huddle with their legal advisers.

Among the residents of Deerfield the news of the Appeals Court ruling created very little stir.

The Dannings read about Deerfield in the New York Times, in their lovely, heavily-mortgaged new house in Westchester County. Bob's promotion had come through in February while the newspapers were full of the legal battle over Floral Park development. Until then he had worked hard on the committee which was trying to raise money to help defray the legal expenses of the defendants. The going had been very tough—the committee had been able to raise only about a third of its $25,000 goal. As soon as he was notified of the promotion, he dropped everything and devoted himself to selling his house. He was afraid to ask for $31,000, the price he had fixed for himself before the interracial housing dispute broke out. But an enterprising agent got him $29,000 within two weeks of the house being put up for sale. Bob reckoned he had broken even on the deal, and was highly satisfied. The new house cost him $39,000.

ask for $31,000, the price he had fixed for himself before

The Dannings don't worry much about integration these days. They're too worried about money.

Joe and Ethel Robbins missed the item about the reversal of Judge Perry's decision. Joe heard about it from a gloating Fred Bernstein. When Joe told Ethel about it, she said, "Oh? Is that good?" Then, she told him about a house she had seen in Highlight Park. "It's an old house, at least compared to this one, and the yard is not as big as I would like. But the rooms, Joe! They're so large! And you should see . . ."

The Robbins are leaving Deerfield.

The Gilberts followed every detail of the trials—in the County Courts, in the Federal District Court, in the Court of Appeals. That is, Frank followed the trials—Paula listened. Frank is a member of the Deerfield Citizens for Human Rights. His major interest, however, is in legislation, in getting the kind of laws passed that would not permit municipal officials to abdicate their authority.

Just after the vote on the referendum, he had read about how Park Forest, also in the Chicago area, had prepared for its first Negro family, which had moved into the suburb on December 28. This was just a week after Deerfield had voted "no Negro families," at least not for now. All the village officials of Park Forest had been involved. Some sort of village human relations group with official status had been organized. The ministers, the chief of police, the village manager—all had participated in a crash program to pave the way for the new family so that there would be no panic selling of homes, no disturbances. And the village president had taken the lead.

Frank had read the news story to his wife with great excitement. This was the way to do things. There had been no organized resistance, the situation had remained calm.

"And the village president, this fellow Dinerstein, he was in there right from the beginning," Frank said to his wife. "Dinerstein? That's a foreign-sounding name, isn't it?" she replied. Frank looked sharply at his wife, then slowly began to smile. He realized that she meant exactly what she had said—no more.

EPILOGUE

Life in Deerfield goes on.

The usual number of junior executives get transferred, sell their homes, and move on. Others move in.

A few residents moved because they weren't too sure Progress Development Corporation would lose its case, and they weren't taking any chance of having Negroes next door.

A few residents moved because they didn't want to live next door to people who didn't want to live next door to Negroes.

Most of the people who lived through the harrowing six weeks between November 10 and December 21, 1959, are still in Deerfield. And property values didn't drop.

During the height of the crisis, in mid-December, a survey of realtors showed that the home prices would hold up. One builder reported that he had had a "pretty good December," including the sale of a $37,500 home only three miles from the Floral Park subdivision. Another home a mile away from Floral Park was sold for $27,000 against a purchase price three years earlier of $28,000.

One of the biggest developers in Deerfield is the Chicago
Construction Company which built the 800-home Deerfield Park subdivision, part of which almost borders on
the Progress Development properties. The vice-president,
Ben Friedman, told a *Chicago Daily News* reporter he had
"sold 10 homes since the announcement that Negroes
might come to live in the village." "Last week," the *Daily
News* article of December 14 continues,

> a home he built was sold for $34,200. The owner paid
> $32,800 when it was built in July, 1956.
> In addition, Friedman pointed out, he is making sales
> of homes which won't actually be built until next spring
> and summer.
> The purchasers, as in the case of other realtors, are
> white. Friedman said that some people are apparently
> confident that the village will block the interracial hous-
> ing by acquiring the land for a park. . . . But he added,
> "I think most people realize that eventually integration
> is going to occur. However, they would like to see it
> happen in a slow, orderly manner, and not with this
> abrupt technique."
> . . . Friedman said he personally investigated a report
> that real estate men would not list homes in the immedi-
> ate vicinity of the proposed subdivision. "I found they
> would—and would be glad to," he said.

The villagers of Deerfield don't show much interest in
the aftermath of the park referendum which blocked—
for the time being at least—the integrated housing projects
at Floral Park and Pear Tree subdivisions.

In the months after the referendum the North Shore
Residents Association was busy trying to raise the $25,000
legal defense fund for its officers. It hadn't been easy. And
the prospect is more litigation, with the Appeals Court
decision calling for a new trial. They don't say much about
integration and Floral Park—the case isn't closed.

After the park referendum the Deerfield Citizens for Human Rights had achieved a membership of over 150, a big gain over the thirty-five who attended their first organizational meeting, but still a tiny fraction of the community. Today the membership is less than 50.

If their number is small, the determination of the Human Rights members is great. The then Chairman Adrien Ringuette submitted a report to his steering committee on January 24, 1960, which was more than a call to action. The report drew on the experiences of communities which had lived through—and survived—the experience of interracial housing. At the same time it summoned the Deerfield Citizens for Human Rights to develop a program which might serve the communities who had yet to experience a first Negro neighbor, and perhaps some say, Deerfield itself.

Report of Chairman

Goals. I would suggest that our principal goal for the coming months is to prepare the village for eventual integration of non-whites after the manner of Park Forest, and thereby to restore the good name of Deerfield. Our "Beliefs and Purposes" as originally adopted on Nov. 29, seem adequate for this purpose. Our first pledge is to urge village officials and citizens to uphold the legal and moral rights of all people to live in Deerfield, and we should continue to carry out this pledge. I suggest we should defer broader human rights objectives in order that we may maximize our strength on this issue.

Obstacles. We have devoted too little time to an analysis of the obstacles we face. Some that come to my mind are as follows:

1. Attitudes toward DCHR. Born in the midst of this integration issue, and not having the support of village leaders, we lack a recognized reputation in the community. Accordingly, there may be some reluctance to listen to our message, especially since the opposition has

branded us as radicals. Our actions sometimes as individuals may tend to reinforce this attitude.

2. Fear of integration. When the Floral Park & Pear Tree developments were announced, Deerfield was totally unprepared for integration. The residents have been beset by fears and humors. Chief among the fears are the fear of depressed property values, the fear that Negroes will eventually overrun the community, the fear that Negroes will not maintain their property, the fear of intermarriage, the fear of loss of social status, the fear of lowered educational standards, and the like.

3. Inertia to change. There is a view rather widely held in Deerfield that neighborhoods should be homogenous. A neighborhood of mixed races is unknown to many and feared.

4. Segregationist Attitudes. In the consternation that followed announcement of Floral Park & Pear Tree developments, leadership in Deerfield passed from the elected officials to the segregationist North Shore Residents Association. The community accepted this leadership, but significantly not under the banner of segregation. Though most people disavow segregation as a philosophy, nevertheless, this alliance is a distinct obstacle.

5. Village leadership. There has been an abdication from responsible leadership in Deerfield. Many of the leaders are opposed to the proposed integrated developments. Except for several of the clergy, few have exercised responsibility to preserve morality and justice.

6. Attitudes toward the builders. The scapegoats of the opposition are the builders, who have successfully been branded. This is an obstacle because inevitably we must defend the right of the builders to build these developments.

Activities. It would seem that we should allocate our resources primarily toward strengthtening our own organization, reaching influential citizens and leaders in Deerfield, and removing the fears of integration among the residents at large. We should not try to change the segregationists, but merely endeavor to isolate them as an effective community force. As to the builders, I think we should consider that their methods are not our primary problem, although we must be prepared to state our position as to their methods. Toward these objects, then, we can plan such activities as the following: (a) compilation of information and data, in cooperation with outside experts, to provide us with necessary ammunition; (b) the use of newsletters to keep our members and friends informed and enthusiastic; (c) a plan for reaching influential citizens and leaders in Deerfield; (d) a general membership drive; (e) establishment of regular contact with all municipal bodies, such as village Board, Park Board, school boards; (f) a plan for inducing village associations, clubs, and church groups, to allow us to make presentations and plan programs at their meetings; (g) a plan for paid advertisements or other means of dissemination of information to the general public; (h) a plan for membership and public meetings of our own organization; (i) a plan for informal home meetings to reach the citizenry in general, and especially those who are eager for information; and (j) liaison with groups outside Deerfield interested in freedom of residence.

The report of the chairman was accepted by a committee still being carried by the momentum of its struggle to defeat the park referendum of only a month before. But the momentum could not be sustained. The members of the board of directors, who today make up most of the membership of the Deerfield Citizens for Human Rights, talk to themselves for the most part. The Catholic Interracial Council of Chicago gave them a citation in 1960 at a large public meeting—in Chicago. The citizens of Deerfield paid little attention.

The *Deerfield Review* continues to serve its readers with

all the news of interest, including the running account of the court proceedings and other matters related to the housing battle. The issue of January 14, 1960, carries as its lead story the announcement that the "Deerfield Defense Fund Goals Is $25,000 For Local Citizens." Below that is the story that "Progress Development Corporation Objects To Deerfield Building Code." On page three is the story that Mrs. Robert E. Jordan, official greeter for Deerfield, welcomed many new families to Deerfield. Of the ten families listed, five came from nearby suburbs, including neighboring Highland Park, two from St. Louis, one from Cleveland, one from Philadelphia, one from New Jersey.

The issue of January 28 reports a new threat to Deerfield property values, contained in a letter by Mrs. Robert D. Winfield. This time the threat is "the encroachment of business into residential neighborhoods with the ensuing downgrading and devaluation of nearby homes." And the threat is again from the "outside," from the "outside businass interests which buy residential property and attempt to have it rezoned for commercial use, thereby increasing the value of their investment at the expense of Deerfield citizens." The letter summons the citizens of Deerfield to battle. "We believe an informed citizenry is a fair and active one. . . . Most of all we believe we can no longer afford to be apathetic. We must become actively interested in all the problems of the residents. When we attain this kind of maturity, our village officials will know our thinking, and their actions can better reflect the desires of the people of Deerfield."

In the February 11 issue Mrs. Jordan welcomed seventeen new families to Deerfield. There was also a brief item announcing that Deerfield resident Donald T. Morrison,

Jr., had been named chairman of the speakers bureau of Americans for Moral Decency, and that a "day-long seminar was held . . . in Chicago where Mr. Morrison arranged for prominent professional men, educators, magazine distributors and retailers to exchange viewpoints on the smut problem." There was also a brief item announcing that John Lemmon would speak in Chicago on "Deerfield —Drama or Dilemma."

In the issue of March 10, the *Deerfield Review* announced with banner headline FEDERAL COURT UPHOLDS PARK AND VILLAGE BOARDS, and in the column, "Your Village Government," Village President Joseph Koss broke a long self-imposed silence:

> For some weeks now this column has carefully avoided mention of the one area of great citizen interest in Deerfield, the court case brought by Progress Developers against the officials and others of the village. Now that the verdict is in, we would like to tell you what the position of the Board of Trustees has been and the reason for that position.
>
> The Board of Trustees and the other Village officials early adopted a policy of counseling rational thought and considered action by all parties of the Village. . . . This position was not the only one open to the Board, and many were the criticisms leveled against the Board because they did not take a stand on the matter. However, it was only by taking this position of study and impartiality that avenues of communication could be kept open with both sides and the Board maintain control of the situation. Once these lines of communication were closed, by the alignment of the Board with one or the other groups, all control would be lost and radical elements might have taken the leadership to the detriment of all in the Village.

But Not Next Door

The issue of March 17 carried Building Commissioner Robert Bowen's anouncement, on the front page, that thirty-six permits for the construction of new houses had been issued in the first two months of 1960. Another item told that fifty-four high school students would take over the village government for one day. "Be perfectly frank and honest in your discussion with these young people," Village Manager Stilphen advised the village officials, "because here is an excellent opportunity for good public relations. They can see through a bluff quicker than we who are older. Here is a grand opportunity to give a group of our future citizens a view of how their local government works."

On March 24 the *Deerfield Review* reported that Theodor Repsholdt would receive a citation from B'nai Torah Reform Temple of Highland Park "in recognition of his deep devotion and exemplary service in furthering the living reality of understanding and the ideals of brotherhood among all men." Repsholdt's pastor, the Reverend Paul V. Berggren, would participate in the ceremonies. It was also reported that Repsholdt was being transferred to the new Deerfield High School in September.

On March 24 the *Deerfield Review* reported Pastor Berggren's announcement that he and his wife would adopt a Negro son.

There was little stir among Deerfield residents when they read the *Deefield Review* of June 30. "Condemnation Suit Settled Out of Court on Monday" read the headline. "All is quiet in Deerfield this week as the months-long controversy over the condemnation suit against the Progress Development Corporation came to a swift finale Monday. The village's suit was settled out of court. The Deerfield Park Board agreed to pay $168,500 for the 22-

acre site that the corporation had purchased for an integrated housing project."

The July 21 isse announced that the Park Board had received full title to and possession of the Floral Park and Pear Tree subdivisions.

A letter from John Hunt, published in the *Review* on August 4 corrected the facts:

> This statement (in the *Deerfield Review*) is to the effect that the park district has paid the condemnation award of $168,500 to our client. This is not so. The money has been paid to the County Treasurer; it has not been accepted by our client.
>
> It is the intention of our client to prosecute an appeal in these proceedings. If the appeal is ultimately successful, then there will be no occasion to accept the money. In such event, the integrated housing developments at Floral Park and Pear Tree subdivisions will go ahead as planned.

On August 25, 1960, the officials of Deerfield changed the signs at the approaches to the village. In 1959 the signs had announced the population of Deerfield as 10,500. Now they read "Deerfield—11,711." The *Deerfield Review* continued to carry the announcements welcoming new families to the community.

On August 25 it was also announced that the Pear Tree subdivision, presumably acquired for the building of a swimming pool, was being plowed up and seeded to be a public playground. As for the two already completed houses on the Floral Park property, one would be used by the park grounds superintendent, the other by the village manager. (The issue of January 12, 1961, announced that the "new park site [was] unaffected" by the ruling of the federal appellate court.)

Christmas, 1960, was a sort of anniversary of the integrated housing battle in Deerfield. The villagers did not
celebrate it particuarly. However, a group of forty Negro
and white youths visited five of the churches in Deerfield
and conducted a "kneel-in" protest during the Christmas
Day services. They then visited one of the condemned
properties and sang carols and "civil rights" songs proclaiming brotherhood. The Deerfield police reported that
the "kneel-in" was orderly and without incident. Most
residents didn't know about it until they read about it in
the newspapers. Very few were pleased. Very few were
angry. Very few cared.

At Christmas time, Morris Milgram sent out a small
four-page letter of holiday greetings to his friends around
the country. It was full of personal news, latest developments in the Deerfield situation, latest undertakings of
Modern Community Developers:
"Nationally, to help in the costly legal battle in Deerfield and similar situations elsewhere, the American Freedom of Residence Fund was organized," he writes, and
lists several distinguished sponsors including Victor
Reuther, James B. Carey, Martin Luther King, Eleanor
Roosevelt, and Norman Thomas. He continues:

> I'll never forget the devoted work of Adlai Stevenson's
> law firm, our midwest counsel, led by tireless John Hunt,
> who despite threats to his family and to our courageous
> builder, Max Weinrib, valiantly pursues elusive justice
> in Deerfield.
> This year models were opened in three developments
> aided by MCD funds, provided by 1,200 investors: single
> homes in Waterbury, Connecticut, and New Castle
> County, Delaware, and co-op apartments in Riverdale,
> New York. In the last two, move-ins have begun. Work
> still continues for a community near Washington, D. C.

Betty found time this year to picket Woolworth's with
CORE; to do volunteer work (as did her dad) for
Kennedy. . . . In addition, Betty, like her brother and
father, collects stamps from everywhere. She continues to
collect autographs, prizing one from the president-elect,
who shares his May 29th birthday with her dad—and
Patrick Henry!

'The daring heart must invade reason with its own
living warmth," writes Bruno Bettelheim in *The Informed
Heart*, "even if the symmetry of reason must give way to
admit love and the pulsation of life." It is this daring
and warmth and love which, it seems to me, is so needed
in the world of today. . . .

To friends near and far, happy holiday!

In January the federal court had remanded Progress
Development Corporation suit back to Judge Perry's
court for retrial with a jury. On April 29, 1961, the Illinois
Supreme Court shattered the hopes of those who believed
the Floral Park and Pear Tree issue had been settled by
the condemnation proceedings in the Lake County District
Court.

The firm of Stevenson, Rifkind & Wirtz had brought
suit, on behalf of Modern Community Developers and
its subsidiary Progress Development Corporation, alleging,
with reference to the Deerfield Park Board, that "public
power may not be used to deny any person the equal protection of the laws." But the Lake County trial court had
refused to hear the civil rights issue in the condemnation
suit. To which the Supreme Court of Illinois replied that
Deerfield must defend itself on charges that it abused
the power of eminent domain.

As reported in the *New York Times* the next day,

the high court said that Mr. Milgram's complaint contained sufficient allegations "to charge the Park Board

with using its power of eminent domain for the sole and exclusive purpose of preventing the sale of homes by (the developer) to Negroes in violation of (the developer's) right to equal protection of the law. . . . We consider such a charge, if proved, to be a denial of the necessary prerequisites to condemnation necessity and public use," the court held.

Deerfield doesn't make big headlines any more. Not many people, in Deerfield or in the nation, seem to be interested in court decisions and the finer points of rulings on appeals. But Deerfield did get into the national limelight again, and this time the issue was not integrated housing. This time Deerfield was clearly and unequivocally on the side of progress (with the small "p"). On the day that the newspapers across the nation carried banner headlines announcing America's successful manned shot into outer space, they also carried a small item announcing that Deerfield's new Junior High School would be the first building in the country to bear the name of the first American astronaut, Alan B. Shepard, Jr.

A few weeks later, on May 24, 1961, Eleanor Roosevelt paid a visit to Deerfield. She was to speak that night in Chicago at a fund-raising dinner at the American Freedom Residence Fund, and had asked to visit Deerfield en route, so that she might see the site of the two model homes (now occupied by two village officials), and to meet some of the people who had worked to allow these homes to become part of an integrated development. At the site she was presented with flowers by children from nearby Wilmot School. Then she went to the home of Karl Berliant, president of the local Democratic club, to meet some sixty pro-integrationist villagers. Complimenting them on their efforts in their own community, she stressed the effect of racial tensions in the United States on the battle with the Communist world for the uncommitted nations. "The effect of your courageous stand is being felt across the world," she said. "The future of your children will be strengthened by your fight."

Later that night, after the dinner in Chicago, new Village President David Whitney visited Mrs. Roosevelt at her hotel. He undertook to correct some of the misinterpretation he felt the village and residents of Deerfield had received as a result of the widespread publicity given to the events in connection with the park referendum.

In a previously all-white suburb of Wilmington, Delaware, a Negro family and three white families moved into Modern Community Developers' first integrated development in a state generally considered to be part of the South. Both Wilmington dailies had given editorial support to this open-occupancy housing. The families moved in—there was no trouble.

Nor was there a ripple of excitement in Deerfield when a Negro minister purchased and moved into the home of Wells Burnette in neighboring Riverwoods, where Harold Lewis also resides.

On October 18, 1961, Lake County Circuit Judge Bernard M. Decker, in a rehearing of the issue, ruled that the Deerfield Park District had acted within its rights in condemning for park purposes the property of Progress Development Corporation, and could take action to acquire it. The November 30th issue of the *Deerfield Review* reported that Judge Decker had refused to modify his ruling upon appeal.

The front page of that same November 30th issue carried the announcement that the "second in a series of three speakers on Communism, sponsored by Deerfield civic organizations, will be presented tonight at 8:00 o'clock in the Deerfield High School auditorium." It reported further that a "record crowd of more than 1,300 persons overflowed the High School auditorium for the first lecture of the series on November 20," which had been given by Mr. Herbert C. Philbrick.

And the same November 30th number of the *Deerfield Review* reported on an inside page: "Americanism Talk at Deerfield High Arouses Protest." The protest had been voiced at a meeting of the Board of Education following the first lecture, and revolved around the co-sponsorship of the series by the Deerfield High School Parent Teachers Association. A letter from the Reverend Russell Bletzer defined the issue: While use of the school building to express such ideas (those voiced by Philbrick) was proper, PTA sponsorship was not.

The United States Commission on Civil Rights, late in 1961, in its report on housing, devoted five pages to the Deerfield Case, as one of four cases involving "affirmative action by local government-action resulting in the exclusion of minorities. . . ."

In January, 1962, the *New Republic* and the *Progressive* carried back-cover ads on Deerfield. They were signed by James H. Slater, President, American Freedom of Residence Fund, and a distinguished board headed by Mrs. Franklin D. Roosevelt and Bishop James A. Pike as honorary co-chairmen.

On January 19, 1962, in the Illinois Supreme Court, John Hunt filed for MCD and Progress an appeal on Judge Decker's second decision. He made clear his clients' determination to go to the U. S. Supreme Court if necessary. Heading the attorneys for this appeal is a volunteer, Joseph L. Rauh, Jr., of Washington, D.C. Rauh, who graduated magna cum laude from Harvard Law School in

1935, was law secretary to Justices Cardozo and Frankfurter, and served on General MacArthur's staff in the U. S. Army in the Southwest Pacific. A leading anti-communist, he is vice-chairman of the Democratic Central Committee of the District of Columbia.

More chapters in the Deerfield story will be written when the builders and the villagers they have named as defendants meet again in the federal courts, and possibly in the state courts. In Deerfield, the residents go about their business as in any other suburban community. A few families move out, more families move in—white families, for in Deerfield there are no Negroes next door.

The newspapers continue to report the changing legal tide—first running in favor of the village, then for the builders, then against the builders. The villagers read the newspapers and stay put. New home-seekers read the newspapers and buy houses in Deerfield.

Deerfield is growing.